When you read *God on the Move* by] every page how much she loves God ar heart for all of her days. Rhonda has given her life to the One she loves, fully surrendering to His mercy, love, and goodness. I hope as you read her book you are inspired to know the Lord, His ways, and His leadings with as much passion.

—Robert Hotchkin
Minister, Author, Media Host
Patricia King Ministries / Men on the Frontlines
www.RobertHotchkin.com

God is always at work—in good times and in bad, whatever the season and no matter the reason, God is at work. Rhonda Kitabjian has captured the essence of how God's love is expressed through strategic timing in all things—every moment having purpose, every prophetic promise finding fulfillment. *God on the Move* is an informative and practical approach to connecting deeply with God and finding fresh revelation in your season.

—Wendy K. Walters,
Motivational Speaker, Master Coach, Publishing & Branding Expert
www.wendykwalters.com

This book is for the disciple who needs encouragement during the "night" and inspiration during the "day." I have known Rhonda and followed her ministry for several years now and have often confided in her with the difficulties that can arise as a pastor. The Holy Spirit has used her countless times in my life to offer me direction, cover me with prayer, and always make the right call at the right time. If you're seeking a greater understanding of God's plan for your life, this book is sure to be the perfect aid in guiding you toward a greater understanding of hearing God's voice and then *acting* on it!

—Reverend C.J. Clevinger
Jackson Bluff Community Church

In these pages, Rhonda Kitabjian reveals steps that will lead you into greater intimacy with our awesome God and into a life that is fueled and propelled by His heart for others. God is on the move, and this faith-filled book will ignite your faith and your passion to move with Him—to *go* and bring life to those all around you, right where you are, with the power, freedom, and love of the Holy Spirit. The time is *now,* and this is for *you!*

—Dr. Michelle Burkett
Director of Patricia King's Women in Ministry Network (WIMN)
www.woflglobal.com

Rhonda Kitabjian is passionate about connecting people to the heart of God. She has led more people to Jesus in the workplace than anyone else I know. Her writings are the perfect reflection of her love and enthusiasm for Jesus paired with her high-impact business acumen. God IS on the move, and this book will help you discover how you can be a part of His movement right where you are.

—Charity Bradshaw
Author, Coach, Speaker, Publisher
CharityBradshaw.com

Ignite Your Faith with a Cloud by Day & Fire by Night

RHONDA KITABJIAN

God on the Move: Ignite Your Faith with a Cloud by Day & Fire by Night
Copyright 2018 by Rhonda Kitabjian

All rights reserved. No part of this book may be reproduced, stored in a retrieval system, or transmitted in any form or by any means-electronic, mechanical, photocopy, recording, or otherwise-without prior written permission of the copyright owner.

Unless otherwise marked, all scripture quotations are from *The Passion Translation*®. Copyright © 2017 by Broadstreet Publishing® Group, LLC. Used by permission. All rights reserved. ThePassionTranslation.com.

All Scriptures marked (NKJV) are taken from the *New King James Version*®. Copyright © 1982 by Thomas Nelson. Used by permission. All rights reserved.

Scripture quotations marked (NIV) are taken from the *Holy Bible, New International Version*®, NIV®. Copyright © 1973, 1978, 1984, 2011 by Biblica, Inc.™ Used by permission of Zondervan. All rights reserved worldwide. www.zondervan.com. The "NIV" and "New International Version" are trademarks registered in the United States Patent and Trademark Office by Biblica, Inc.™

Scripture quotations marked (NLT) are taken from the *Holy Bible, New Living Translation*, copyright © 1996, 2004, 2015 by Tyndale House Foundation. Used by permission of Tyndale House Publishers, Inc., Carol Stream, Illinois 60188. All rights reserved.

Scripture quotations marked (NASB) are taken from the *New American Standard Bible*®, Copyright © 1960, 1962, 1963, 1968, 1971, 1972, 1973, 1975, 1977, 1995 by The Lockman Foundation. Used by permission.

This book is dedicated to the Holy Spirit who has continually spoken to me about the Father's plans for His children, especially in this season. His incredible patience and love for me as I wrote this book guided me daily to communicate and impart His wisdom. I am forever grateful to God my Father and my Lord and Savior Jesus Christ, who left the Holy Spirit to minister to me for such a time as this!

"But when the Father sends the Spirit of Holiness, the One like me who sets you free, he will teach you all things in my name. And he will inspire you to remember every word that I've told you" (John 14:26).

Acknowledgments

I would like to thank my husband and family for always supporting me as God gives me directives to do His work on this earth.

I would also like to thank Andy Sanders for his guidance and wisdom from the Holy Spirit to help me along in this journey. He showed me what it's like to have support from a publisher and man of God who intimately seeks His heart on a daily basis. Thank you for seeing God's plan for this book in its infancy stage.

Also, I am forever grateful to my prayer team—Susana, Sharon, Kate, and Jennifer! Without their constant prayers and covering, this book may not have been created and birthed. They are the epitome of *love, joy*, and *spiritual wisdom*. God has gifted me with their warrior-like persistence, and for that I am beyond blessed.

Contents

Foreword		11
Introduction		15
Chapter 1	God's Word as Prophecy	23
Chapter 2	Meditating on God's Word	35
Chapter 3	Crying Out to God	45
Chapter 4	Focus on Jesus	59
Chapter 5	Focus with Spiritual Eyes	69
Chapter 6	Focus with Spiritual Ears	81
Chapter 7	When God Speaks, Don't Keep Silent	93
Chapter 8	Posted at the Watchtower	105
Chapter 9	No Shortage of Faith	113
Chapter 10	Serving the Body of Christ	123
Chapter 11	Employed by God	133

Foreword

Foreword

You're in for a real treat! I know, you're not easily impressed and sometimes you're overloaded with things and voices vying for your attention. But you've picked up this book, and I can assure you, things will change in your life as you read it.

We live in a world of superficiality, filled with shallow relationships and sometimes shallow commitments. This is also seen in the church. But the times are changing. God is calling His people to go deeper and come closer to His burning heart of love. People everywhere are starting to get it. We need to give ourselves fully to something. For believers, that something is Someone, and His name is Jesus.

God has given us so much. His gifts, wisdom, power, and glory are all available to us. In fact, they live within us. I really believe we are entering a time when every believer is activated in their gifts. Every believer is about to be motivated to live all-out for Jesus. Another Jesus Movement may be in the works in this generation. You are born for such a time as this. It's time for you to follow the teachings of Jesus to be His instrument, His vessel of honor, and to carry the glory of His name to the nations. As you are immersed into the life of Christ, you will be taught by the Spirit how to manifest Him each day.

We want the real, don't we? Many people have asked me over our forty years of ministry: What is the secret? What keeps you going and burning for God? The answer, for me, is simple. Remain faithful to what He has taught me. I long to be obedient to Him to the end of my days. All I have to do is wake up each day and spend myself on Him!

It is time to choose God and allow Him to have first place in your life day and night. As you set your eyes on Christ, making Him your horizon, your eyes begin to focus and you see Him more clearly and your destiny more distinctly. Rhonda Kitabjian will help you. She is gifted by the Holy Spirit to take you into that realm where everything and everyone bows before the Lamb of God.

Do you want to hear God's voice and know that He is speaking to you? Do you want to begin to understand your dreams? Are you burning with a passion to know God and enter into union and communion with Him? You will find the secrets tucked inside these pages. Filled with examples of how to lead people to salvation through everyday encounters throughout your life, *God on the Move* will show you how. You are about to become a massive blessing to many as you learn these secrets of how God wants to use you day and night in the lives of others!

You will be delighted to read Rhonda's testimony of how God has spoken to her and raised her up to be a voice for this generation. Her history as an Armenian Christian will touch you deeply. You'll discover that the first Christian nation on earth was Armenia! What a rich treasure God has deposited in her heart—generations of Armenian blessings given to us through her writings.

I was especially moved by her description of how the living Word of God can penetrate our hearts and actually become a part of us. Her steps? Observe, interpret, apply, and respond! It doesn't get better than that. Loaded with truth, this enjoyable book will fill you and give your life spiritual fuel to move forward. And at the end of your journey through this book, you will know God has a plan to use you to equip and encourage others.

So, get ready. Open your heart as you open this book and expect great changes in your life! Read it with joy. Read it with anticipation. And make sure you get an extra copy for a friend. This is too good not to share! May God Himself bless you day and night until you are fully transformed into that beautiful, radiant image of Jesus. Amen!

—Dr. Brian Simmons
The Passion Translation Project
www.thepassiontranslation.com

Introduction

Introduction

How God Gave Me *God on the Move*

Don't you just love how God works in our lives? I am not sure if you have ever had the Lord come to you in a dream, but I have been asking the Lord to do exactly this for the past five to seven years. Before I lay my head down to sleep, I ask the Lord to come to me in my dreams and reveal only what He wants me to know for His kingdom on earth to expand for His glory. One night, I woke up gasping, which woke my husband from his very sound sleep. He was concerned and said, "What's wrong?" What he didn't know was how the Lord had visited me in my sleep and whispered in my ear.

Now, don't be jumping to conclusions about "How can God visit you? You would be blinded by His presence, wouldn't you?" I didn't physically see the Lord, but I felt His presence and I can say without a doubt it was the Lord's voice. As He whispered in my ear, He said "The name of your new book is...." That's when I woke up with a large gasp, mostly because His voice was so close to my ear. As quickly as I heard Him speak, that's how fast I couldn't remember anything He said to me about the name of the book. When my husband was fully awake, he asked me what was wrong, and that's when I began to cry!

Have you ever had an encounter with the Lord where you wanted to have the experience of the encounter all over again? You loved how you felt in the encounter, and in the tenderness of that moment you never wanted it to end. This is the exact feeling I had when I woke up. I think I must have cried off and on for over a week because I was so sad that I couldn't remember the words God spoke to me. I thought to myself, *How could this happen? Why did it happen?* These are the questions I may never have answered; however, being the researcher and learner that I am, I studied the many ways God speaks to people in dreams and why sometimes we don't remember them. What was truly amazing about this experience was what I learned. God sends us dreams and sometimes He then keeps them hidden, only to bring them back to remembrance at a time He appoints. Job 33:15-17 explain this to us:

> He speaks in dreams, in visions of the night,
> when deep sleep falls on people
> as they lie in their beds.
> He whispers in their ears
> and terrifies them with warnings.
> He makes them turn from doing wrong;
> he keeps them from pride (NLT).

It seems there is a treasure of gold buried deep in your soul, and only your spirit and God know its location. Thank you, Jesus, for your Word, which confirms what we need to know. In fact, Luke 8:17 tells us, "For all that is secret will eventually be brought into the open, and everything that is concealed will be brought to light and made known to all" (NLT).

I stood upon the Word and thanked God for coming to me in my dream. I was excited to know that in the appointed time He would open my eyes and ears to hear what He wanted revealed for His glory. A few months later, I woke up from my sleep early in the morning reciting the words, *night and day, day and night*. I kept saying them over and over without stopping. *Lord, why am I repeating these words out loud?* I wondered. At that moment the voice of the Lord came to me, "Look up the words and see what my Word says." Immediately, in the very early hours of the morning, I got out my computer and searched the Internet for Bible verses containing the words "night and day." To my amazement, there are over 429 occurrences of the word *night* and over 1918 occurrences of the word *day*. The combination of the two words occurs over 53 times. I researched further and discovered information regarding the way time is reckoned by the Jewish people.

Introduction

In Jewish time, the day begins with the onset of night (the appearance of the stars) followed by the morning (which technically begins with the appearance of the North Star). According to some Jewish teachers, night and morning begin with sunset and sunrise respectively. For that is how the Torah describes it: "And there was evening and there was morning, the first day."

For this reason, the Sabbath begins on Friday night and ends with the appearance of the stars on Saturday night. The same is true for the major holidays such as Passover, Sukkot, Shavuot, Rosh Hashanah and Yom Kippur, the fast day of Tisha B'Av, and Hanukkah and Purim.

By starting day with night is a metaphor of what life is like. Our lives start in the womb in darkness, bursts into brightness of light, and then at the end settles into the grave back into darkness, followed by a new beginning in the brightness of the new life of eternity.

The Lord gave me the phrase *night and day*, and with it, so much clarity to understand what it means in the Bible. But it wasn't until this book was in the final stages that He spoke again through a prophetic friend of mine named Jennifer. As we were praying for the book title, the Lord showed her how He guided His people (the Israelites) with a pillar of cloud by day and a pillar of fire at night. (Exodus 13:21). She said, "I feel the Holy Spirit wanted to share this verse with you for the title." As I prayed about this prophetic word and the title, it became very clear in my spirit God wanted His people to know how He is the one to guide us day and night, night and day. The cloud and the fire were also God's way to guide, protect, and often speak to His people in a supernatural way. Fire and smoke (cloud) signals were already being used during that time by army generals, and here we read in Exodus how God Himself wanted His people to know He was the commander and chief to lead His people (army) out of Egypt into the Promise Land.

I was amazed by what God had shown me. I knew this book was to be birthed for the season God's children are in right now, knowing that God will use His pillar of cloud by day and fire at night to show that He is undeniably on the move to awaken His people (you and I), bringing us back to the heart of our Lord and Savior Jesus Christ.

What God Is Doing in This Season

This period of time we are in is unlike any other in recorded history. As I write this, we are celebrating the 500-year anniversary of the reformation of Martin Luther, as well as a fifty-year jubilee (see Leviticus 25:8-13); and Israel will be celebrating seventy years since it became a nation (May 1948).

In view of that, how can we embrace this movement of God right now? We need to start looking all around us to see how God is on the move for the billion-soul harvest prophesied by Bob Jones in 1975. We need to realize that the Creator of the universe doesn't sleep and His timing is perfect, as it says in 2 Peter 3:8-10.

What do you think your role is in this movement of God? Are you part of God's army that is preparing the fertile soil with seeds and fertilizer, or are you sitting back and waiting for God to send you a message to move? We need to look at our lives as a service to God and, in doing so, start fulfilling the God-given destiny that has been appointed to your life.

I believe the words *night and day* are meant to get deep into your spirit. God will show you as you walk with Him that His army of warriors never rests and is constantly working on your behalf (see Romans 8:28). Did you know God appoints people all over the world to do His work for the glory of heaven to be fulfilled? Right now, there are men and women working to bring love, peace, and comfort to the lost, the homeless, the motherless, and the orphaned. While you sleep, God is at work in the world. This means your chosen destiny is vital in the kingdom, because we are all working together for God's purposes to be fulfilled. Not only in our own lives, but in the lives of those God puts in front of us. Isn't it amazing how during different seasons of our life, God will always move us into unusual places for His own strategic plan? The plan He gives you may not make sense to your carnal mind. Or, maybe he gave you a dream years ago that He is resurrecting right now. Either way,

Introduction

His love for you is endlessly deep, and He only wants it to grow deeper still.

I pray this book encourages you as a believer to keep pressing in to God. He wants you to feel, taste, see, and hear His powerful presence moving in your spirit. As you press in to His words and as they penetrate deep in your soul, you will start to see a change in your inner spirit man. Get ready and hold on tight to your Bible; you are about to engage in the ride of your life. May this book serve as a tool to help you prepare during this season and beyond. I pray acceleration in your spiritual giftings as night and day, day and night God moves in your life.

Chapter 1

God's Word as Prophecy

Chapter 1

God's Word as Prophecy

A joyous blessing rests upon the one who reads this message and upon those who hear and embrace the words of this prophecy, for the appointed time is in your hands (Revelation 1:3).

What Is Prophecy?

To understand prophecy, we are going to look at how prophecies were written in the Bible by prophets appointed by God. We know these prophets had to hear from someone, and that someone is God. The Greek word for prophecy defined by Strong's Concordance states that it is "the gift of communicating and enforcing revealed truth."[1] When I first came to know Jesus as my Savior, I had never heard of the word *prophecy*. I did, however, know that Jesus was a prophet and the Son of God. As I grew in my knowledge of the Bible, I began to learn about spiritual gifts the Lord gives us (see Romans 12; Ephesians 4; 1 Corinthians 12–13). I understood from Romans 12:6 that being a prophet or speaking prophetically to someone is a gift by which the Holy Spirit speaks through us.

There are many reasons why God would want to prophesy to someone. The main reason I discovered is to encourage or edify that person regarding what they are currently doing, which is bringing glory to

---

1. Strong's Concordance, G4394.

God's kingdom. It can also be used for conviction, the way the Lord convinces a person to look introspectively at their life.

Different prophecies in the Bible were used to usher in the testimony of Jesus to others. As it says in Revelation 19:10, "At this I fell facedown at the angel's feet to worship him, but he stopped me and said, 'Don't do this! For I am only a fellow servant with you and one of your brothers and sisters who cling to what Jesus testifies. Worship God. The testimony of Jesus is the spirit of prophecy.'" This means the testimony of Jesus in Revelation points us back to Christ's teaching while He was on the earth. Remember, a prophetic message is not meant to draw attention to the person speaking, but it is meant to serve as a marker, pointing people's attention directly back to Jesus.

The Encyclopedia of Biblical Prophecy by J. Barton Payne states that there are 1,239 prophecies in the Old Testament and 578 prophecies in the New Testament for a total of 1,817 prophecies! When I was researching for this book, I was astounded to discover how many prophecies were written in the Bible. What's even more exhilarating is how God wants us to use our prophetic gifting to bless others. I also believe God wants you and me to understand the role of prophet in order to be aware of true prophets, as well as discern those who are walking around as false prophets. In Matthew 7:15-16 Jesus explains how to look for false prophets, saying, "Constantly be on your guard against phony prophets. They come disguised as lambs, appearing to be genuine, but on the inside they are like wild, ravenous wolves! You can spot them by their actions, for the fruits of their character will be obvious. You won't find sweet grapes hanging on a thorn bush, and you'll never pick good fruit from a tumbleweed."

In helping you learn a little about false prophets, I am going to share what happened to me not too long ago. A person contacted me unexpectedly, claiming they were an apostle and prophet, and said that one of my "friends" told him about me. Mind you, this person did not know me at all, but continued almost every other day to make some kind of connection with me for about a week. During our conversations, I had an innate feeling that something wasn't quite right, as this person said things that didn't sit well with my spirit. I stayed in prayer, asking

God's Word as Prophecy

God to reveal to me if these were conversations I should be having, as they were getting personal with my family, knowing the names of my children and husband. God answered my prayers, as things changed rather rapidly after that first week. This person began to share things about their personal relationship with their spouse, which made me feel sick to my stomach. They also kept telling me to place the title of apostle and prophet before my name during most of our conversations. They said that I *needed* to let the world know *who I am*. As soon as these words came out of the person's mouth, the Holy Spirit quickened my spirit and told me, "Rhonda, close the door on this conversation."

The "friend" who knew this person said they believed everything this person said was *truth* and would never think anything was wrong with the things they proclaimed. Knowing something wasn't sitting right in my spirit (as the Holy Spirit gives us the spirit of discernment), I prayed, not just alone, but with other respected pastors and ministers in Christ, confirming what I needed to do, which was to close the door on this connection, just as the Holy Spirit directed.

This person continued to contact me by calling me, texting me, and messaging me on my Facebook posts. During that first week, they kept pestering me with high-pressure tactics, telling me to change my title on my business cards, as well as encouraging me to get ordained as a prophet, as others had been ordained by them. I researched their background and found this person had no credentials and was not under any umbrella of a legitimate ministry. Also, there was no fruit from this person's ministry and I was seeing how they lured other women who were new in their ministry to essentially *follow* them and be ordained by them. Peace came upon me immediately when I closed the door to the connection.

Because of my intimate relationship with the Lord and knowing who I am in Christ, I was grateful to avoid trouble that could have occurred. My "clue" about this person came from knowing the verse we just read in Matthew 7. Seeing no fruit from this person's life became the major red flag in my spirit, and in situations like this it can be yours as well. It is important to consider who you are talking to when someone wants to prophesy into your life.

At a conference recently, I got a little card after someone prophesied over me and it said, "Write out your prophecy word for word. Do not make major decisions based on one prophetic word alone. Test prophecy against Scripture and the character of God. They require faith and obedience on our part to unfold." Any word that does not line up with the Word of God will fall to ground and sink like it landed in quicksand. It will not bear fruit—it's as simple as that.

In Deuteronomy 18:18-19, we read of the importance of God being the one to raise up a prophet. The Lord told Moses, "I will raise up a prophet like you from among their fellow Israelites. I will put my words in his mouth, and he will tell the people everything I command him. I will personally deal with anyone who will not listen to the messages the prophet proclaims on my behalf" (NLT). From this verse we should understand the importance of recognizing that it is God alone who will raise up a prophet. People cannot raise up a true prophet, and those who appear because of man's approval will quickly fall to the ground and not produce fruit for God's kingdom. This is what could have happened to me. I recognize that I have prophetic giftings, but God will tell me if He has given me the role of a prophet and if I am to put this title on my card or promote myself to the world. For now, I am waiting on the Lord and thankful for the title I have as a daughter of the King of kings.

We have been given additional information to determine if a prophet is from God or is an imposter in Jeremiah 28:9: "So a prophet who predicts peace must show he is right. Only when his predictions come true can we know that he is really from the Lord" (NLT). As I mentioned earlier, the fruit of a prophet's words are in the way their predictions come to pass. Researching the word of God will help you in hearing a true prophetic word while also helping to grow your own giftings in the prophetic.

Why Is Prophecy Important?

Some people wonder why prophecy is important in today's world. Often, I hear from Christians who are new in the faith—or even from those who have been walking with the Lord for years—say to me, "Why do we need prophecy now? Can't we just look at God's prophetic words

God's Word as Prophecy

from the Bible?" The answer is yes. However, we need to know why God gave us prophecy so we can operate in the newness of this season. Therefore, let's understand a bit more about the importance of prophecy.

First, prophecy is God's way of protecting and guiding His children. He does this several ways. One method God uses is to deliver dreams at night so we can recall them in the morning. I personally have had the Lord send me the same dream on three separate occasions in a very short time frame.

In one of my dreams, the Lord showed me a gray wolf and I was aware of the cunning ability the wolf has; but in my dream, I sprayed the wolf's nose and he couldn't smell me. The next dream that came to me was about several wolves attacking animals, but I was able to see what they were doing through a protected glass. In my third dream, a wolf was trying to follow me in a car, but we were able to outrun it in the woods. All of these dreams took place over a period of one year. As I looked to the Lord for answers about the meaning of gray wolves as well as the actions I took in these dreams, the Lord revealed what He wanted me to know and brought all the pieces together like a puzzle. Imagine if I never wrote these down? It is so important for you and I to write down any dreams the Lord sends us. Also, we should always be questioning what God wants you to know from your dream and try to understand if your dream is a warning or a prophetic dream for the future.

The second way prophecy is important is that God, through His prophets, speaks so that His children will prosper (see 2 Chronicles 20:20). A prophet is meant to uplift the church, so as you listen to the prophets you will be blessed and prosper according to God's word. We as believers are called to be prophets for His kingdom, especially during these days of great harvest. As I was learning the gifts of the spirit, I came to understand that I too was given this gift. However, just as a gift that is unopened will remain in the box, so too will your gift of prophecy remain unopened unless you give that gift to others. What I want you to grasp here is the need to exercise this gift by practicing it on a daily basis. You can practice giving a prophetic word with your closest family or with friends first. Don't worry if you get it wrong or if they tell you it doesn't make sense. Keep practicing. It's like riding a bike; you may not be able to go more than fifty feet at first, but after practicing you can ride for miles without trepidation.

When I hear from the Lord, I confirm what He speaking to me by reading His Word. Sitting with Jesus, reading the Word, and listening to His voice are your first steps. Then you should be writing down what you hear. If you see things come to pass, amen. If not, don't relinquish your gift from God. On the contrary, press in even more. Often, I have had some of my closest, trusted Christian friends listen to specific prophecies spoken over me. I even ask them to seek the Holy Spirit to confirm what I've heard. You should always have mentors or trusted believers around you, as there is safety in a multitude of counselors. Another word of advice is to not fall into the trap of scrutinizing every word in your prophecy. As an alternative, I would like you to ask, "What is the main point of the message; what is the Lord saying to me?" Simply look for the take-home message instead of dissecting each word. The Lord will reveal all things in His time.

Prophecy is also about preparation. Not only does it prepare us to meet the Lord at any time, but it also prepares us for some potential future events.

Sometimes a prophetic word can be called a word of knowledge. It is a word from the Lord given to a worshipper to impart to the people. This can happen through speaking in tongues, which would require an interpretation from another believer, or it might come directly in the person's known language.

We impart this word when we have gained access to God's deep knowledge and wisdom. Speaking a "word of knowledge" to encourage or uplift His children. We have the opportunity to inspire and empower others with God's thoughts and dreams when we seek Him for a word of knowledge.

I have been studying words of knowledge for quite some time and have discovered it is exciting to tap into prophetic words for those around me. I have so many testimonies of exercising this gift. I was attending church one Sunday, and a friend of mine came up to me and gave me a hug. As we started to talk, the Lord prompted me to tell her that He would never

God's Word as Prophecy

leave her or forsake her. You see, she had a rare form of cancer that the doctors said was incurable. We had been believing and praying for her to be healed since she was diagnosed. After I asked her that question, she looked at me with tears in her eyes. She said she was searching out a psychic to foretell her future in order to know whether she was going to live or die. I was shocked that she was considering this, because she was a very faithful believer and servant of God. However, I knew it was not a coincidence I saw her in church that day and felt the Lord prompting me to tell her that specific word. Through our conversation, we were able to pray about how our God who created the universe knows all things, and He would never leave her. We also prayed for the devil to get behind her and flee. She felt immense peace that day as she left the church. She continued to live out each day as if it were her last, enjoying every moment the Lord gifted to her. This testimony illustrates how we never know what God's intentions are when He gives us a word for someone. His ways are always higher than our ways, and His thoughts are not our thoughts (see Isaiah 55:8-9). Lean upon Him as you seek out His word to share with those around you, demonstrating and communicating the light of Christ.

God Works with Holy Spirit

When you walk with the Lord, you are in service to Him, using all the gifts of heaven given to us as believers. The New Testament church (the body of Christ) is called to be a prophetic people from its very birth. Everyone is called to use this gift. Have you been practicing this gift given to you? If not, now is a perfect time to understand all that God intends for you to possess and use for His glory. I would say the most important Scripture regarding prophecy is from 2 Peter 1:20-21: "You must understand this at the outset: Interpretation of scriptural prophecy requires the Holy Spirit, for it does not originate from someone's own imagination. No true prophecy comes from human initiative but is inspired by the moving of the Holy Spirit upon those who spoke the message that came from God." I feel relief when I can read Scripture and know the Holy Spirit is required for me to speak in a prophetic manner. It's not me people will be looking at in amazement; it will be Jesus to whom they will give the glory and praise.

God on the Move

One day, I was at the airport returning home after attending a Jesus Conference in Orlando, Florida. I was so full of God's glory and power of the Holy Spirit that I couldn't help but sing to the Lord as I was walking through the airport, as well as when I sat down and waited for my flight back to Boston. Lots of people came up to my friend and me asking if we were in a gospel choir or a church group. Some people even asked us to be quiet, in an unkind fashion. When those people yelled at me to be quiet, I remembered what I learned from Todd White at this conference. He said, "Once you realize you are accepted in the beloved, you will never feel rejection by people. Why? Because no one on this planet can ever take away what they didn't give you." I heard his words ring in my heart and thought about this angry person, knowing he was not angry with me but his anger was simply because he didn't know Jesus. With that in mind, I kept on singing praise and worship songs to God. Just as I was finished my song, an older man sat right next to me. I looked over to him and he said, "Are you one of those Jesus people?"

I replied, "You mean the ones who go all around and share the love of Jesus with whomever they meet?" He looked at me and said, "Yes." He proceeded to tell me of his life in Eastern Europe where he decided that God doesn't exist. He then shared with me how he was a proclaimed atheist and looked at me for a reaction. I politely said to him, "That's OK, God still loves you."

With that, he looked at me, even more perplexed, and went on to tell me he was a scientist. As he was speaking, I was getting excited in my spirit. He then proceeded to tell me how he could prove that God doesn't exist. What he didn't know in his own spirit is how God had been preparing his heart for a radical encounter with Jesus. I explained to him how I was also a scientist, and this is precisely why I love the Lord. I asked him if he would like to do a science experiment with me right now. As scientists are generally curious, he said yes. I asked to hold his hands and told him to repeat after me. I then proceeded to lead him into the prayer of salvation. After the prayer was finished, the man had tears in his eyes and he reached out to hug me! He said with such joy and peace in his voice, "I will go home to my country and tell everyone what happened to me today, and how you are responsible for

God's Word as Prophecy

this momentous day in my life." I quickly told him how I would much prefer he tell his family that Jesus loved him so much He sent me there that day in order for him to enter the kingdom of God.

It's amazing to see how the Holy Spirit worked in this man's heart. I was sure He would work in his whole family when he arrived. This transformation took place because I stepped out in faith to speak by the power God gave me with the Holy Spirit. As I stated earlier in the chapter, "the essence of prophecy is to give a clear witness for Jesus." The result of prophecy is clear. It is revelation from Jesus, predominantly with the purpose of expanding His kingdom on earth. As God works in you and you work with the Holy Spirit, people will begin to testify of their love in Jesus poured out from within you.

Seeking the Wisdom of God

Hearing a prophetic word from God allows us to release the meaning of what we receive to whomever the Lord wishes. I am always in prayer over any word the Lord gives me, seeking His wisdom, and I want to encourage you that the Lord will always confirm His word. As it says in 2 Corinthians 13:1, "This will be my third trip to you. And I will make sure that by the testimony of two or three witnesses every matter will be confirmed."

Remember, just because you sense, hear, or see something does not mean it is supposed to be released. Timing is key, as well as staying connected to the source of God's voice. Many times, if a word is spoken out of season it will have limited, if any, anointing and can actually hinder what Holy Spirit is doing. That is why we need to continuously seek the wisdom of God when we hear from the Father. As I minister to people, I am in constant communication with the Holy Spirit to ensure what I am hearing is not only correct, but also whether or not He wants me to reveal all I am hearing from Him. I had a recent experience where I was at a new hair salon in my area. The man who was cutting my hair was very kind and pleasant. As I sat, the Lord asked me to share a prophetic word with him. As I prayed and knew it was for that time, I told this young man how people were going to be looking up to him as a teacher and he would be known in the industry. Surprisingly, he told me that he already was teaching, but he had never had anyone tell him something so encouraging from the Lord. I asked him if he read the Bible or attended church. He said he had never gone to church nor owned a Bible. I told him that next time I came in I would bring him a Bible. So the next time I went in, I brought the Bible with me, but as I was grabbing it off my car seat, I felt the Lord say, "Do not give it to him now. He needs to know me as savior."

Oh my gosh, I thought. *OK, Lord.* So, I proceeded to go into my appointment, and as I sat in my chair he began to tell me about his mother. She apparently is a psychic, and he was excited about the word I gave him at my last appointment. He called his mom and told her about the word I shared with him. He said his mother was so excited to hear that God loved him and had that specific word for him. As I listened to him, I knew I wasn't supposed to say anything about his mother's searching for the supernatural by doing psychic readings. God knew exactly what He was doing and who his mother was, which was why He wanted me to say those words from the heavenly Father. Seeking wisdom in what you hear is vital to growing your faith as well as the spiritual gifts God has given you. Each time I go get my hair done, I am patiently waiting for the Lord to reveal His word to this young man who is a child of God.

As you seek wisdom from the Lord night and day, feed upon this word from Proverbs 4:6-7 and watch God move in your life to give out what you have sought from Him.

> Stick with wisdom and she will stick to you,
> protecting you throughout your days.
> She will rescue all those who passionately listen to her voice.
> Wisdom is the most valuable commodity—so buy it!
> Revelation knowledge is what you need—so invest in it!

Chapter 2

Meditating on God's Word

Chapter 2

MEDITATING ON GOD'S WORD

Keep this Book of the Law always on your lips; meditate on it day and night, so that you may be careful to do everything written in it. Then you will be prosperous and successful (Joshua 1:8 NIV).

The Principal of Meditating on God's Word

When we meditate on God's word, we begin to focus and remember what He says. I love how in Joshua 1:8 it communicates the message of remembering the Law day and night; essentially, when you wake up and when you go to sleep. When we do this, the Bible promises we will be prosperous and successful. Why would anyone want to give up such a blessing?

There was a time when I used to believe in following the way the world does things. I accepted Christ at the age of twelve, but didn't start to truly understand His Word until the age of twenty-four, when I got baptized in water and professed my faith in Jesus. It was amazing to be in front of over 500 people testifying my love for Jesus. When I told them out loud about my salvation and got immersed in the water, the Holy Spirit came upon me. It was at that moment the Word of God became alive in a brand-new way. It was at this point that I began to be guided by His voice and direction instead of the world's.[2]

When giving God my time in prayer and meditation to read His Word, my day is full of goodness, with added surprises. I start to see miracles all around me as well as blessings that follow me. Another way to say this is that I feel God's presence all day long. Now, you may be saying you don't have time or your day is super busy with "to-do" tasks. Believe me, I get it. I have three children and a husband as well as a dog that needs lots of attention. When you think this way, you mind gets stressed about the many things you must do instead of looking to the one source of your strength—Jesus. He is the well of water that springs up within you to refresh your inner soul (see John 4:14) and your outer body to go about doing His work for the kingdom. You must look to Him to be refreshed daily, and you do this by setting aside time to sit at His feet.

When my children were growing up, I attended a mom-to-mom Christian support group. They taught me to prepare my children daily with God's Word before they left the house and went to school. In class, they explained to us the importance of God's Word being used as armor for our children. This teaching really struck my heart. The leader explained we should ask the Lord in prayer which Bible verse He wanted to impart upon my children for the school year. She then directed us to have them memorize and declare the Word out loud as they left home each day.

The Lord gave me Romans 12:2 for my oldest daughter, Sophia. It says "Do not conform to the pattern of this world, but be transformed by the renewing of your mind. Then you will be able to test and approve what God's will is—his good, pleasing and perfect will" (NIV). This verse has been a pivotal word in her heart. She has fed upon, leaned upon, and relied upon this word. It has held her up and given her strength when the world seemed to be crashing down on her. Through this one verse, my daughter could stand

---

2. If you haven't taken the step to be baptized, the Bible teaches us that this is what we are to do in Matthew 28:18-19, "Then Jesus came close to them and said, 'All the authority of the universe has been given to me. Now go in my authority **and make disciples of all nations, baptizing them in the name of the Father, the Son, and the Holy Spirit.'"** Some say baptism after you ask Jesus into your heart is like a marriage. You may ask: Who am I marrying? Jesus, of course. I believe this step is very special to His heart, and once you experience it I have confidence you will feel the same way.

against the world's ways with confidence and boldness. She understood that her mind needed to be renewed each day. What does that mean? It means that you are gaining a new perspective. When you renew your mind, this will bring your will into agreement with the Father's will. You do this by filling your mind with His Word by reading, discerning, recalling from memory, praying, communicating, and even singing to your heavenly Father. You begin to think in a way that pleases Him, and His ways become your ways.

The verse spoken over my daughter every day as she was growing up was very powerful in her life. She told me recently how she considers this to be her personal verse from God. I'm amazed when the Lord gives a word or a verse for someone and it truly resonates with their hearts so much that they feel a divine connection to their heavenly Father. The promise of 2 Corinthians 5:17 tells us what happens when we accept Jesus, "Therefore, if anyone is in Christ, the new creation has come: The old has gone, the new is here!" Even though we are a new creation, we may not realize we need daily renewal in our minds. Romans 12:2 in *The Passion Translation* states that we are to "Stop imitating the ideals and opinions of the culture around you, but be inwardly transformed by the Holy Spirit through a total reformation of how you think." When we don't stop imitating the world, we continue to live in it. The first part of the process is to seek the Lord; the second part of transformation is when we embrace the change within ourselves. When you meditate on God's Word each day, you will be able to embrace the newness of transformation in your life with ease and joy.

God's Word Penetrates Our Hearts

Life in America is considered one of the busiest for men and women today. In fact, when you ask the question, "How are you doing today?" most Americans will reply, "Very, very busy." You may be wondering how you would be able to set aside time with God each day when there are tasks and responsibilities to complete. The first suggestion I have is to examine your current schedule. That includes writing down when you are waking up and what time you plan to go to bed. Realistically, you will find a block of time in your schedule that you can spend at least fifteen minutes with the Lord. When you include Him in your daily routine, you will see the effects of spending time with Him almost instantly. You see, the world is constantly throwing curveballs at us, trying to distract us from our mission or destiny. We know Jesus called us "lights of this world," but how can a light function without fuel? It can't. You need fuel to survive. This only comes from feeding upon the Word of God daily as if your life depended on it, because it actually does!

Therefore, how does God's Word penetrate our hearts? We must look to Hebrews 4:12, where it says, "For we have the living Word of God, which is full of energy, and it pierces more sharply than a two-edged sword. It will even penetrate to the very core of our being where soul and spirit, bone and marrow meet! It interprets and reveals the true thoughts and secret motives of our hearts." God gave us free will, we have a choice in whether we want to pursue Him with our heart and soul or not. When you make a choice not to walk with your heavenly Father, you essentially are forfeiting the blessings that come from being with Him night and day. You will start to feel your desires more closely aligned with the world than with Him. Yet when you choose to walk with the Lord, people all around you can see and feel the love that exudes from your being with Him. The fruit of the spirit in you is seen and felt when people encounter you. Isn't that amazing!

Here are some simple steps you can use every day as you meditate on God's word.

Step 1: Observe

Step 2: Interpret

Step 3: Apply

Step 4: Respond

In the first step, as you read a Bible passage make an **observation** about who wrote the book you are reading. Then, write down who this writer is writing to, which you can generally find at the beginning of the book. Finding out this information helps you get the context of the time in history. If you do this at the beginning of your meditation, you will be enlightened to the freshness of God's Word. **Interpreting** what God was trying to convey in the verse or passage can help you understand more about it and discover its lessons for the season you are in as you read. **Applying** the Word of God helps you to become empowered by the power of Jesus living in you in order to change circumstances or relationships, which can have a tremendous effect on your life. The last step is **responding**. Here, think about how you will respond to life's circumstances. This is very important, because I believe this piece is critical to your relationship with the Lord and with those you love. Your response is an indication of your spiritual walk with Jesus. Each verse you read is to get you closer to the Lord and to enable you to know how to respond to certain situations or circumstances. Using these steps daily will help you to walk in greater faith, as you will be more prepared for what God brings your way.

Distractions from the World

When I say the word *distraction*, what first comes to your mind? Children, work, family obligations, or your own self-preservation? No matter where we are in life, distractions will come our way and try to take us off the path the Lord is leading us on in this season. You may be saying to yourself, "I can't help getting distracted, Rhonda; I have two children, an aging parent, and a spouse to take care of!" I understand, and I totally empathize with you as well. Hence the reason God wanted to instill in His children the action of meditating on His Word. Life will happen, you will get pulled in many different directions, but God is still with you and He will never leave you or forsake you (see Deuteronomy 31:6).

While I was raising young children, I was pulled in a million directions. The Lord constantly reminded me, if I wanted to wake up and feel His presence, I needed to spend time with Him in the early hours. That is what motivated me to start my prayer journal, which is now a twenty-year daily routine. I look forward to my alone time with the Lord, where I know I will be refreshed in His presence. You see, I decided to put God first. This is the primary key to removing distractions. Whatever you give priority to will have a profound effect on your life. God is peace, joy, and love (see Galatians 5:22). He will fill your spirit with those spiritual-fruit attributes.

Let's say you're also a full-time employee or you own your own business. How would you keep distractions from your time with God in this situation? Well, it just so happens I have worked in the business world for over twenty-five years. What I would recommend is that you make it a priority to have alone time with the Lord, either while you're driving to work or during your scheduled breaks. I did this on a daily basis at each of my places of employment. I would also keep Scripture verses on my desk or have them on my computer so I would get fed by the Word every day.

What kind of priority are you giving the Lord in your life right now? If you're not making a place or time with Him, then you may not be able to hear the purpose or plan He so desires for your life. Martin Luther, one of the pivotal figures of church history, gave detailed instructions on how to meditate when he said, "You should meditate not only in your heart, but also externally, by actually repeating and comparing oral speech and literal words of the book, reading and rereading them with diligent attention and reflection, so you may see what the Holy Spirit means by them."

I want to share another testimony, where God gave me direction while I was in preparation to launch my consulting business. One day, I felt God speaking to me regarding the official launch of my new business. Some people hear God in a voice that penetrates their heart, and I am one of those people. I heard the Lord speak urgently to my heart about going to the bank so I could set up my business account. As I conversed with the Lord, as I normally do, I agreed with Him. However, I then began to go about my day and the thought left my mind. Many distractions kept coming up, and I was operating as if I never heard from Him. The Lord is quite humorous with me because as I was cleaning up some paperwork, two of the exact forms needed for a bank to open a business account fell right on the floor in front of me. Just then, I heard the voice of God speak to my spirit again, saying, "Are you going to go now?" You see, there were many distractions going on in my life that day, but God's voice prevailed over all of them.

I told my daughter to jump in the car because we need to go to the bank right away! When I got there, a young man helped me open the account while asking me questions regarding my business. He then proceeded to write down names and email addresses of people I needed to connect with for my business. That is what I call divine favor and perfect timing. What I have learned from walking with the Lord is that He is the door-opener of your life. He will either open the door for your future and His plans or He will keep the door closed for your protection and His timing. The door that opened for me that day has led to countless new relationships and connections. It even has resulted in me becoming a new board member for the YWCA, serving women to embrace change for justice in this world. Through my testimony, you can perceive how the Lord will confirm His Word by what you read as well as through the time you spend in meditation with Him. Bible reading, prayer, and meditation on Scripture are absolutely essential to know God's will. It's even more important in growing in your faith when there are distractions all around you.

God's Law Is Truth

Do you happen to know any of God's laws? Many of us who grew up in the church learned the Ten Commandments from the book of Deuteronomy. This is the Law of Moses given to him at Mount Sinai from God. What I would like you to grasp here is how God sent His only Son Jesus to teach us the law of grace, which is summarized in words that Jesus spoke in Matthew 7:12: "So in everything, do to others what you would have them do to you, for this sums up the Law and the Prophets" (NIV).

What did Jesus commission His disciples to do when He left this earth? He said to love others. Is it really that simple? Yes, it is. In fact, Paul said in Romans 13:9-10, "For the commandments, 'Do not commit adultery, do not murder, do not steal, do not covet,' and every other commandment can be summed up in these words: 'Love and value others the same way you love and value yourself.' Love makes it impossible to harm another, so love fulfills all that the law requires." We know that by grace we have been saved, as it says in Ephesians 2:8. Therefore, it is only by God's grace we get to enter into this kingdom of heaven on earth without doing any works. I am amazed how God arranges things in our lives and gives us everything we need without us working and striving for it the way the world does. Don't get me wrong—you need to apply for a job to show you're interested, but I have found that in my own life God has sent me jobs for which I have never applied. He also does this when He wants to open doors for you. My point is that you don't need to do anything to earn the love of God. He loves us because we are His. This also doesn't mean we shouldn't understand the Old Testament or know the history of why God did what He did. On the contrary, we are part of the history of Christ. When you accepted Jesus as Savior, essentially the disciples and forefathers who fought to bring the truth of Jesus become part of you and your history.

God on the Move

Joshua speaks of the importance of God's law as truth by stating in Joshua 1:8, "This book of the law shall not depart from your mouth, but you shall meditate on it day and night, so that you may be careful to do according to all that is written in it; for then you will make your way prosperous, and then you will have success" (NASB). If we take this word as truth and love others as ourselves, our way will be prosperous and filled with much success. I don't know about you, but that is exactly what I want for my life and the life of my family. You may be asking, what if the way I am walking in now doesn't seem prosperous even though I am following the Law? My answer to you is do not lose hope. For if you continue to follow the truth of God's law and seek His heart in everything you do, then in God's timing you will reap what you sow (see Galatians 6:7). Meditation is the act of deeply allowing the Word to penetrate in your heart so you can speak it out loud to your spirit man. Finally, you can apply it to your own life and circumstances so it will not depart from you. Remembering all that God has done for you (praise) and will do for you in the future (thanksgiving) will keep you focused on Him rather than on your circumstances. Through this process of meditating on His Word, you will start to see the movement of God in your life, and the truth will set you free.

Chapter 3

CRYING OUT TO GOD

Chapter 3

CRYING OUT TO GOD

Don't you know that God, the true judge, will grant justice to all of his chosen ones who cry out to him night and day? He will pour out his Spirit upon them. He will not delay to answer you and give you what you ask for (Luke 18:7).

Restoring Our Spirit

When most of us hear someone crying out loud there is a reaction that happens in our spirits, which causes us to stop what we are doing and care for that person. God created us to be emotional beings, so these emotions can trigger in us a response of empathy. Crying out is usually a response to a specific emotional event, or it can arise from feeling powerless in a particular moment. When we cry out, it is an intense petition to the Lord to restore our spirit. I think of it as a last resort for the Lord to intervene in a circumstance or situation we need to resolve.

The power of crying out to God draws us closer to Him. As we step into a deeper relationship, His voice becomes clearer to us. In a relationship with the Lord, you communicate in such a way that He hears your voice as a loving daughter or son. He has the ability to bring restoration to the area of your life that needs it most. You may be thinking, *How can the Lord restore what was stolen from me or my family?* This is where I love pointing people back to the Word of God; I don't ever rely on my own senses or understanding. What I do rely on is how the Word of God speaks truth and sets people free. It's a promise God gave us.

In the book of Joel 2:25-26 we read, "The Lord says, 'I will give you back what you lost to the swarming locusts, the hopping locusts, the stripping locusts, and the cutting locusts. It was I who sent this great destroying army against you. Once again you will have all the food you want, and you will praise the Lord your God, who does these miracles for you. Never again will my people be disgraced.'" I just love this verse, because it tells us no matter what you have been through, if the enemy has stolen something from you or your family, God's Word promises He will restore what has been taken from you. What's even greater about this verse is how you will praise the Lord your God, who does these miracles for you.

There are times in my life when I have literally cried out to God, believing He would remove a particular pain-point in my spirit. As a mother to three children, I just wanted God to fix things or make them better. My son is the middle child who is a very loving young man, but when he was small it was a challenge to keep him in line. There were many times he would think, even as a five-year-old, that he was the boss. Now, don't get me wrong, I know God created him to be a leader. As he was growing up, God had shown my husband and me how to discipline and train him in the way he should go as a leader in God's kingdom. However, that did not mean as a mother I didn't have days when I was tired of training a leader for God. Those were the days I cried out to the Lord, asking Him to restore my spirit to be in line with His will, giving me the peace I so longed for. His answer always came.

As we cry out to Him, He will lift the aches of our heart to heaven and direct us to focus on Him rather than our circumstance. There are times when I have lain prostrate on the ground, crying out to God for help. It is in these times He comes to me and speaks in a gentle and loving voice. I feel His arms wrap around me, and He says, "Rhonda, I love you. Lean on me and cast your burdens at my feet." At that moment, I feel peace come upon me and lift my spirit. All the thoughts and worries are put aside in order to bring my focus back to Jesus. This is exactly what God

Crying Out to God

is calling us to do in this season. His presence is enough for us to live and breathe each day, and we need to trust Him in the process of living.

Have you ever felt as if you needed a miracle to restore your life? When my children were young—all under the age of seven—I was praying to the Lord for Him to show me His will for my life. I will never forget this day. As I was crying out to Him, I felt the tangible presence of God all around me. Just then, in my spirit I heard the Lord say to me, "As I moved the Israelites out of Egypt into the Promised Land, so I will also take you from this place to the Promised Land I have for you." In my spirit, I felt I was to start packing my home. Immediately, I got boxes and started packing up my dining room with the articles I wanted to take with me to the Promised Land. When my husband came home from work and saw me packing, he said, "What are you doing?" That's when I told him what the Lord had spoken to me about the Promised Land.

Not long after that we began looking at new homes. I prayed the Lord would show me exactly where this Promised Land was that He desired us to move to, and I went to an open house where I felt the presence of God immediately. As I walked in this home, He said, "Here you are." The only problem was, the house already had ten bids on it, and a person who was expecting to move in. When I came home to tell my husband, he looked at a photo of the house and said, "This is our home." I agreed, but told him it already had buyers ready to purchase it. Sure enough, it was sold the next day.

Because God showed me the type of home He was giving us, I got all of our finances in order to be ready for the actual Promised Land God was taking us to. About a week later, as I was praying in the early morning hours, I went on my computer and a home popped up on my notifications. Would you believe it was the same home God had me walk in, where He said, "Here you are"? On the listing, it said "BOM" which means "Back on Market." I immediately called my realtor, and amazingly, she didn't even see the posting listed. I told her that we were going to be the ones to buy this home. However, when she called me back she said that, once again, it already had eight offers on it. It didn't matter to me if there were one hundred offers; I knew the promise God had given me and I wasn't willing to let that promise go. We went to see the house that day and we were the last ones to look before the owners planned to make their decision. My husband and I prayed that the Lord's will would be done. Sure enough, two hours after our offer went in, the realtor called me back and said we were the ones chosen to buy the home. God came through and His promise was fulfilled.

Now, this is where crying out to God became more prevalent. You see, we didn't have our current home on the market, and because of the recommendation from our mortgage specialist, we decided to do a bridge loan. This is when a bank temporarily loans you money to bridge the gap between the sale of our old home and our new mortgage, in the event our current home doesn't sell. There were incredible risks in doing this bridge loan, however, this is where our faith was tested. Just as the apostle Peter walked out on the water at the invitation of Jesus, Peter was "afraid; and beginning to sink he cried out, saying, 'Lord, save me!' And immediately Jesus stretched out His hand and caught him" (Matthew 14:30-31 NKJV). We too can see God save us as He hears us cry out to Him, and in turn He will respond to us.

My husband and I did cry out to God because it was two months of paying two home mortgages, two heating bills, and two electricity bills on one income. We didn't know whether we were going to have sell our new home and move back into the previous one or what was going to happen. I kept telling my husband that the Lord spoke to both of us and we were obedient to Him, so we needed to stand on His word.

This is when the Lord showcased His power and love for my husband and me. That night, I had a dream. In my dream, I saw my realtor at a round table saying to me, "Guess what?"

I replied, "What?"

She said, "I have sold your home."

At that moment, I started crying out loud; the tears wouldn't stop.

She looked at me and said, "Why are you so sad? This is a happy moment."

I said, "I am happy. I'm happy because the Lord heard my prayers and He answered them."

Crying Out to God

Then she asked, "Would you like to know how much I sold your home for?"

"Of course!" I said.

She said, "I sold it for $420,000."

Just then, I woke up. Several hours later, I received a real phone call from my realtor. She said, "Rhonda, you're not going to believe this, but I just got an offer on your home!" The phone practically dropped out of my hand and I started to cry. "Do you want to know how much the offer is for?" she asked.

"Yes, I do."

It is for $420,000!"

These are the times when the enemy tries to put self-doubt, self-pity, and anger in your heart. The enemy knows the time to move in to destroy what the Lord is doing, but God is greater, and His power will overcome any words the enemy uses to lie to you. We always need to remember that it is a spiritual battle we face while on this earth (see Ephesians 6:12).

Glory be to God for His faithfulness to His children and the love He feels for us as we cry out to Him. God restored our spirits and our finances; He reformed our way of thinking about how He does things; and He brought refreshment of living water into our lives through what He did. We can see through this testimony and the testimonies of people in the Bible that the act of crying out to God gives way to an internal revelation in our spirit. It can cause us to be humbled, knowing that we desperately need the Lord, and we need faith to believe our cries will be heard by our Father in heaven.

God's Response

I want to share with you some real examples of biblical characters who cried out to God and instantly heard His response. Through these stories, you will see the response they received from your faithful and loving Father. The first testimony is where God revives someone who is pronounced dead. In 1 Kings 17:20-22, we read that Elijah cried out to the Lord, and God revived a dead child. "Then Elijah cried out to the Lord,

God on the Move

'O Lord my God, why have you brought tragedy to this widow who has opened her home to me, causing her son to die?' And he stretched himself out over the child three times and cried out to the Lord, 'O Lord my God, please let this child's life return to him.' The Lord heard Elijah's prayer, and the life of the child returned, and he revived!" (NLT).

We can see in this verse how the power of prayer caused God to respond and revive this child who was essentially lifeless. I had a real-life experience—not where God revived someone who was dead, but where God responded to my desperate cry after I had two miscarriages. These miscarriages happened following the births of my first two children. You see, God knew my desire was to have three children, yet here I was after two miscarriages without my third child in my arms. It can be very difficult to overcome feelings of loss, or that perhaps having a third child was not part of God's plan for my life. However, I stood daily on God's Word knowing He would grant me the desire of my heart (see Psalms 37:4) and that His plan for me was perfect. It wasn't until I had come to peace with God and had exhausted my breath from crying out to Him when something finally happened. Yes, you guessed it. I got pregnant with my third child. Her name is Ava Lily which means breath of life and beauty! She is absolutely a breath of life to our family, and I thank God for her and all of my children every day. God's response was to answer my prayer and bring a new life into our family.

In the book of 2 Chronicles, Jehoshaphat had also cried out to the Lord, and God delivered him from death. "So when the Aramean chariot commanders saw Jehoshaphat in his royal robes, they went after him. 'There is the king of Israel!' they shouted. But Jehoshaphat called out, and the Lord saved him. God helped him by turning the attackers away from him" (2 Chronicles 18:31 NLT).

Jehoshaphat cried to the Lord by acknowledging his fault in going with this wicked king to war against the word of the Lord by his prophet and also by desiring mercy for the same. We need to be reminded from this story that when we partner with evil, there are consequences we will face. Here we read how God was with Jehoshaphat, and through his cry to the Lord God responded to bring His faithful people out of the difficulties they put themselves in. The Lord has our hearts in the palm

Crying Out to God

of His hand and He can instantly rescue us from the evil that seeks to destroy us. This word is very comforting to me. It is a message of trust and faithfulness to the Lord our God who created us for a divine purpose.

There was a time during my younger years when I was in between jobs, so I decided to go on a cruise. None of my friends were available with such short notice, so I went alone. During one of the excursions, I was given a few too many "free" drinks. I had met a lot of people on the trip, and they quickly became my "friends." However, no one was really watching out for me or had my best interests at heart except for Jesus. This one night, I decided it was going to be fun to jump into a four-foot pool head first. Was I thinking logically? No. Did anyone warn me to not jump in? No. When I jumped in head first, I heard my chin hit the gunite bottom of the pool, and I felt my teeth crack. My first thought was that I may have broken my chin, teeth, and neck. As I came to the surface, no one was even paying attention to me, and of course there were no lifeguards present. I pulled my arms to the side and prayed to God that someone would see me bleeding and rescue me. Thankfully, the Lord quickly heard my prayer and responded. A married couple I had met came running over to me and pulled me out of the pool. Unfortunately, I did crack my teeth and my neck was badly hurt, but all the praise goes to God that I did not die that day. I know in my heart God sent His angels and they must have pulled me up an inch or two so I didn't crack my neck and die instantly or have a permanent cervical injury. Statistics show one in ten people who dive the way I did usually end up in a wheelchair, paralyzed for life. God saved me that day, as He did Jehoshaphat when he cried out to Him.

There are many examples in the New Testament where Jesus cried out to God, but in Luke 8:23-24 we read how the disciples cried out to Jesus while they were in a storm, and instantly Jesus calmed the sea.

> One day Jesus said to his disciples, "Let's get in a boat and go across to the other side of the lake." So, they set sail. Soon Jesus fell asleep. The wind rose, and the fierce wind became a violent squall that threatened to swamp their boat. The disciples woke Jesus up and said, "Master,

> Master, we're sinking! Don't you care that we're going to drown?" With great authority Jesus rebuked the howling wind and surging waves, and instantly they stopped and became as smooth as glass.

This is a great testimony to us as believers, because it shows how we too can fall prey to the enemy's plan for fear and worry to creep into our souls. Imagine if you had Jesus with you and a storm came. Would you also be quick to see only with your natural eyes and start losing your faith? Seeing how the disciples, who were with Jesus day and night under His teachings, could quickly fall for the scheme of the devil, causing them to doubt their safety with Christ, reminds us also to call upon Him who can save us. Have you ever been in a life storm where in the natural it seemed all was going against what you knew God had said to you? May this word be confirmation to your spirit, knowing we carry the same power of Jesus to rebuke the storms and command them to be calm. God's response is to answer your call.

Reluctant to Cry Out

Are you ever hesitant to cry out to God? Sometimes I can be, if I am too immersed in my problem or difficulty. When reading how David cried out to God in Psalms 55:17, we are encouraged in our souls. Here he writes, "Every evening I will explain my need to him. Every morning I will move my soul toward him. Every waking hour I will worship only him, and he will hear and respond to my cry." I can tell you from experience, there are many reasons that prevent God's children from reaching out to their heavenly Father. If you think about it, it is similar to one of your own children who may at times (especially during puberty) feel they are more than capable of doing everything themselves. Therefore, they do not share with you about the peer pressure they are under or the temptations that come their way. They don't want to share their feelings because of fear of being exposed or having to turn from their sin. This is a web the devil likes to weave around God's children, to make them believe in the lies that will prevent them from going to Jesus, where they can be set free.

CRYING OUT TO GOD

In raising my own children, I have taught them to know and believe there is nothing so shocking or traumatic that it would cause me to not love them. Just as Jesus loves us unconditionally, we too as parents need to love our children unconditionally. Teaching our children to turn their hearts toward Jesus and cry out to Him will keep them in line with the truth of love. The main plan of the enemy is to steal, kill, and destroy; so it befits the devil's description to use others in such a way that will make them reluctant to turn to the Lord, or even to their parents, for help. We are ambassadors of Christ; therefore, we are to turn back to Him in order to carry the good news of Jesus to this world. Don't be reluctant today to cry out to the one who can bring you peace, joy, and love!

> We are ambassadors of the Anointed One who carry the message of Christ to the world, as though God were tenderly pleading with them directly through our lips. So, we tenderly plead with you on Christ's behalf, 'Turn back to God and be reconciled to him" (2 Corinthians 5:20).

The Root of Bitterness, the Blessing of Forgiveness

> For day and night your hand was heavy on me; my strength was sapped as in the heat of summer (Psalms 32:4 NIV).

In this verse from Psalm 32, David cries out to God in excruciating pain and guilt. David felt the hand of God upon him, but not in a light way. Let me reiterate—we are the ones who put guilt on our hearts because we are unwilling to ask God to forgive us for something. Here in this verse, David felt this physical pain, which stems from unforgiveness. When you put guilt on your heart, you too may feel this kind of pain and it may manifest itself in sickness or illness in your body. You see, the root of bitterness can take hold in your spirit man and actually grow. The word *bitterness* denotes the disappointment and anger we feel when we are treated unfairly. We can learn what God has to say about this word from Deuteronomy 29:18: "I am making this covenant with you so that no one among you—no man, woman, clan, or tribe—will turn away from the Lord our God to worship these gods of other nations, and so that no root among you bears bitter and poisonous fruit" (NLT). This means we are the ones who bring this bitter fruit to life. It cannot take root without us planting it there.

Several years ago, I had a manager who was, shall we say, very full of himself. This in itself didn't bother me or make me think less of him, because I know who I am. I also knew that God loved him, but he didn't know it because he had never been exposed to the gospel. Anyway, there were so many times when he showed disrespect, acted immature, and even put me down on a daily basis. These actions can wear on your spirit man day in and day out if we are not careful. This is exactly what happened to me. Without even realizing it, I developed a seed of bitterness against my manager. One day as I drove home, I was listening to a sermon that taught how our soul can get wounded and cause us to have a root of bitterness, which can cause sickness in your body. At that very moment the Holy Spirit brought my manager to the forefront of my mind. I knew instantly I needed to ask for forgiveness and be cleansed of this root of bitterness in my soul. The prayer I said was something simple like, "Dear Jesus, I ask You today to forgive me for the bitterness I feel toward my boss. I desire, Lord, for my soul to be healed of this root of bitterness and cleansed by the blood of Jesus." Right there in my car, I instantly felt forgiveness and I started to cry as the Holy Spirit mended my soul.

We are not the only ones to go through this or unknowingly plant this root. Hebrews 12:15 states, "Watch over each other to make sure that no one misses the revelation of God's grace. And make sure no one lives with a root of bitterness sprouting within them which will only cause trouble and poison the hearts of many." Mankind has been placing this root in their souls since Adam and Eve, but the amazing thing about this is how God wants you set free from sickness, disease, and ailments by confessing your negative thoughts or feelings toward another person. Until you confess your sins to the Lord, you will continue to feel discomfort, which is the Lord's guidance to freedom through forgiveness, springing from confession and repentance.

When understanding true forgiveness, I believe humility can play a part in our lives where we are not hesitant to cry out to God because of our self-absorption. Instead of an "I-should-be-first" attitude, we will be thinking, "Lord, show me how to serve others before myself." When we are consumed with ourselves, we are not able to put God first—or others for that matter. C.S. Lewis once said true humility is "not thinking less of ourselves, but thinking of ourselves less." Some would call our self-absorption spiritual blindness. There's another word for spiritual blindness and it's called pride. When pride creeps in, you can be prevented from crying out to God. When you are prideful, you tend to always put the focus on you. However, the Lord desires for us to put our focus on Him. When we are prideful, we tend to be blindfolded to the love the Father holds for us. The purpose of these blindfolds is for us to continue our sinning or hiding a sin we've committed. If we stay prideful, this blindness will keep us from acknowledging our own faults. Unfortunately, we will continue to think we are right when everyone around us knows we are wrong. We will look at other people's faults as things that need immediate repair; however, our own faults will be quickly dismissed.

I have some hope for you today, as there is a way to break pride in your life so you can be free to reach out to God. First, you must admit you're a sinner and in need of Jesus. Then, you need to remember that God formed you and you were created for His purpose. That purpose is to serve the Father, obeying Him and praying that His will be done on earth as it is in heaven. It's that simple.

Let's look to the example Jesus gave us when He humbled himself. Jesus consistently demonstrated a spirit of profound humility, saying that He came "not to be served but to serve others and to give his life as a ransom for many" (Matt. 20:28 NLT). On His last night with the disciples, He took a towel and basin and washed their dirty feet (see John 13:1-11), instructing them to follow His example of servanthood with one another (see John 13:12-17). This is the example we are to follow in order for pride to be removed from our lives and allow humility to sink deep in our soul.

I love this quote from D.L. Moody: "I firmly believe that the moment our hearts are emptied of selfishness and ambition and self-seeking and everything that is contrary to God's law, the Holy Spirit will come and fill every corner of our hearts; but if we are full of pride and conceit, ambition and self-seeking, pleasure and the world, there is no room for the Spirit of God. I also believe that many a man is praying to God to fill him, when he is full already with something else. Before we pray that God would fill us, I believe we ought to pray that He would empty us. There must be an emptying before there can be a filling; and when the heart is turned upside down, and everything that is contrary to God is turned out, then the Spirit will come." Let's pray right now for God to empty us today so He can immediately fill us with His love.

The Bible clearly states we are to forgive others for our own benefit and well-being. "When you forgive this man, I forgive him, too. And when I forgive whatever needs to be forgiven, I do so with Christ's authority for your benefit, so that Satan will not outsmart us. For we are familiar with his evil schemes" (2 Corinthians 2:10-11 NLT). When I forgave my manager, the chains that were holding me back from experiencing love were broken, allowing God's kindness to flood my heart. There is a very clear reason we are to love one another—to represent our King, knowing Jesus first loved us. Take time today to ask the Holy Spirit if you may have a root of bitterness toward anyone that is causing unforgiveness. Seek God with humility; then, by the power and blood of Jesus, ask for that root of bitterness to be taken from the inner part of your soul in order to be set free and forgiven forever!

Chapter 4

Focus on Jesus

Chapter 4

FOCUS ON JESUS

This is why you must stay alert: because no one knows the day your Lord will come. But realize this: If a homeowner had known what time of night the burglar would come to rob his house, he would have been alert and ready, and not let his house be robbed. So always be ready, alert, and prepared, because at an hour when you're not expecting him, the Son of Man will come (Matthew 24:42-44).

Preparation for the Lord's return

The phrase "prepare the way" can be defined as creating a path for a person which makes it easier for them to walk in or down. Jesus tells us how to prepare the way in the book of Revelation. In Revelation 2:5, He explains three steps we need to take—*remember, repent, and return* to Jesus. "Think about how far you have fallen! Repent and do the works of love **you did at first.** I will come to you and remove your lampstand from its place of influence **if you do not repent**."

I'm not sure how many people, on a daily basis, think about one day the Lord returning to earth, but I know there are many who would welcome His return. An example of this expectation is to look at my aunt and uncle who are missionaries. They have told me many stories of their trips to some of the poorest parts of India and Myanmar. As they preach the message of salvation to hundreds of people who have never heard of Jesus, it is alarming how many want Jesus to come right then. You see, when you are stripped of everything, living on dirt floors, eating one cup of rice a day for a family of four, you tend to welcome the Jesus you have come to know in your heart. In America, even the poorest places are not as poor as the places I have described. Statistically, the median income of America is about thirty thousand dollars, and in Mexico it's only five thousand. We may know of Jesus here in the states, but there are many who haven't repented yet in preparation for the Lord's return, and they tend to forget Jesus in their day-to-day living.

The way of *remembrance* is to look back when Jesus became Lord over your life. Then, keep that fire burning in your heart the way it once did by taking action each day to shower love on those around you. If you're not a believer, you first need to *repent* and ask Jesus into your heart. In understanding the steps we take, in knowing how to prepare for Jesus' return, we ourselves must return to Christ. The footnotes in *The Passion Translation* explains the verse in Revelation 2:5 saying, "Return to your passion for me that motivated you at the first." What I believe this means is when I first accepted Christ into my heart, the love I felt from the Father was so overwhelming I could not contain it. I had to share His love with those around me. Many came to know Him because of the overflow and passion which poured out of me. As we wait for the Lord's return, bring your mind, body, and soul back to that place when He filled every void in your heart, and all you felt was immense love that you couldn't contain.

I would also suggest forgiving those in your life whom you feel an offense against; as we read previously, we do not want the root of bitterness to stand in the way of our relationship with Christ. In Colossians 3:13, Paul writes how important it is to forgive grievances against others. This is significant because if you do not forgive others, you will stay imprisoned to the past, and this is exactly where the enemy wants you to stay—in the past. However, the Bible encourages us that when we become new creations, the old is passed away and the new has come upon us (see 2 Corinthians 5:17). Then, as we embrace our newness, we can expect to win people to Jesus. Paul even expands upon this and urges us,

Focus on Jesus

"Now, even though I am free from obligations to others, I *joyfully* make myself a servant to all in order to win as many converts as possible" (1 Corinthians 9:19). This is part of every believer's calling—to win souls for the kingdom.

All of these steps bring you into a closer relationship with God, and you are also advancing in your preparation to meet the Lord one day. As I prepare, I don't actually start my day saying, "How am I going to prepare for the Lord's return?" However, I do wake up and read the Word, pray, and ask Him what He wants me to do for His kingdom that day. Is this actually preparing for His return? Yes. I am walking out the Lord's plans each day, so it is in line with the Word of God on preparation. What I also consider is those around me in my realm of influence whom I can share the love of Jesus with through my life. If you are working in any job, you can share Jesus by being an example of His love. If you're a stay-at-home mom or dad, you can meet with other parents and share with them what Jesus has done in your life and in your children's lives. The point is, wherever you are you can have an influence to change the environment around you, and this is preparation for the Lord's return.

John the Baptist, who was Jesus's cousin, was born to prepare the way for Jesus. He was born as the one to bring repentance to the hearts of God's people. In Matthew 3:1-3 (NLT) we read:

> In those days John the Baptist came to the Judean wilderness and began preaching. His message was, "Repent of your sins and turn to God, for the Kingdom of Heaven is near." The prophet Isaiah was speaking about John when he said,
>
> "He is a voice shouting in the wilderness,
> 'Prepare the way for the Lord's coming!
> Clear the road for him!'"

John knew his role was to prepare for Jesus who was coming after him. I believe the people were ready to receive and welcome Jesus because their hearts were already softened to receive the words of Christ. The same is true for you and me when we are speaking to others about their own preparation. God prepares the hearts of those who are about to encounter us because we carry Jesus in us and His light shines brightly through us. John the Baptist was chosen to help build the Father's kingdom by preparing the way for Jesus. We are also chosen to help build the Father's kingdom by helping people know more about Jesus and the ways of redemption.

Follow the Lord's Leading

In our quest to be ready, it's important to make sure our hearts are continually submitting to Jesus. When we do this, we essentially are saying, "Whatever you ask of me, Lord, I will willfully obey." Remember, when you first asked Jesus into your heart, you made a statement of your faith in Christ, knowing you needed a savior to give you eternal life with Him in heaven. This was your first act of submission to the Lord. Not only is submitting to God an act of obedience, but it also demonstrates your trust in Him. As you obey Him, He continues to give you promptings to walk along the path that was created for you from the beginning of your life. The Bible gives us so many ways to follow the Lord's leading. In Genesis 12:1, God spoke to Abraham, "The Lord had said to Abram, 'Leave your native country, your relatives, and your father's family, and go to the land that I will show you'" (NLT). The same is true for you and me. He will show us where He is leading us and all we need to do is follow Him.

A couple of years ago, I was let go from my position as the director of product at a healthcare company. What was amazing about this turn of events was how the Lord showed me six months prior to my being let go that He was going to be taking me out of this job. During that time, He proceeded to tell me how I was going to be a consultant for business leaders. I have this written in my prayer journal as a reminder of how I hear from God. Even though I had heard from the Lord and I was preparing my heart for this move each day, when the day came without any warning from my manager, I felt sadness in my heart that I had to leave all the people I had come to know and love. There were over fifteen people who got saved at this job, and I was mentoring them daily in their walk with the Lord. It was my daily ministry. I was a little nervous because even though God had told me where He was taking me, I didn't know the exact path. It was an unknown data point for me. However, as I left my job that day and was driving home crying, it was then the Lord spoke softly to my heart, "You are free, Rhonda!" Free? I didn't fully grasp the message God was sending me.

It seemed glorious to not have to work a full-time job on top of my other responsibilities. But it did take me over nine months to comprehend the true meaning of "freedom." It was so hard for me to let go of what I once knew. It was especially difficult to trust God for what He knew was best for me and my life in order serve Him. Today, I am pleased to say I am truly free. Free to do God's work in the capacity He has called me to. My business, Royal Business Consulting, has helped many business leaders gain a clearer focus by expanding their vision and focusing on their mission. Since the time I was let go, I have been faithful to the Lord by letting Him be my CEO. We meet each day and I allow Him to direct my steps and lead me day by day, minute by minute. This is the truest sense of freedom that Jesus wants us all to know and experience each day as we simply follow the Lord's leading.

The Teaching of Jesus

How do you take the walk of Jesus and follow His ways on a daily basis? Looking back to how Jesus taught His disciples is one of the best ways we can emulate His teaching in our own life and share it with those whom we are in contact with day to day.

Here are several ways you can follow Jesus in your own walk:

1. Go to the heavenly Father daily and **be immersed** in His anointing in order for your vessel to be full (see Acts 10:38).

2. Jesus was a servant leader, so we too must **serve others** to show the love of Jesus that lives inside of us (see Mark 10:4)5.

3. Use your gifts to **mentor** those around you (see Luke 19:5).

4. **Train other leaders** and have them go out two by two in order for them to encourage one another (see Mark 6:6-7; Luke 9:2).

God on the Move

I can tell you firsthand how lonely it is to serve God as a leader; but then again, who said you need to be alone in your calling? In my own company I am the only one who reports to work each day, and I am accountable to God and myself. But to be encouraged in this position, I look at how Jesus went to be with the heavenly Father alone, and when He came down from the mountain He was joined by His disciples or by those who needed healings or miracles. You also can serve the Lord by observing how Jesus taught His disciples the power of unity. Together we can accomplish so much.

One of the most popular Bible verses that teaches this is Proverbs 27:17: "As iron sharpens iron, so a friend sharpens a friend" (TPT). Purposefully, I have joined Bible studies, gone to workshops, participated in Christian business groups, and even have Bible studies at my home. We can choose not to be alone in this journey by joining with those who can be an encouragement in our walk with the Lord. In each of these actions, I am learning from someone or I am mentoring someone who needs help. Either way, you are doing exactly what Jesus did in His ministry and that's something to celebrate!

As we work together to accomplish the goals set before us, we also need to incorporate what is considered our responsibility for the lost. Jesus spoke a lot about this as it was His desire for everyone on earth to know who the heavenly Father was and why He sent Him to earth. To this regard, we must look to the salvation message.

In 1 John 5:11-12 we read, "This is the true testimony: that God has given us eternal life, and this life has its source in his Son. Whoever has the Son has eternal life; whoever does not have the Son does not possess eternal life."

Jesus is the way and the truth and the life. There is no other way to heaven without Jesus. He spoke often of this while on earth, and He trained His disciples to teach this all over the world. Each of the disciples went two by two, teaching others the message of salvation. This is how Christianity spread across the world so quickly.

Speaking of spreading across the world, the Armenian people were forced to leave their land because of a genocide that occurred in 1915.

Focus on Jesus

I'm not sure if you could tell from my last name, but if anyone has the letters "IAN" or "YAN" at the end of their name means they are of Armenian descent. Not only am I Armenian, I also of Finnish nationality. Not many people know this, but Armenia was the first Christian nation.

> In 301 Gregory [Lusavorich] baptized Tiridates III [who was the king of Arsacid Armenia] along with members of the royal court and upper class as Christians. King Tiridates III issued a decree by which he granted Gregory full rights to begin carrying out the conversion of the entire nation to the Christian faith. The same year Armenia became the first country to adopt Christianity as its state religion.[3]

Do you think Christianity would have spread had Gregory not stepped out to baptize the king? I think not. We too are commissioned to bring the Good News of Jesus wherever we go and baptize those who believe in the name of the Father, Son, and Holy Spirit. When I think of this commission, I realize I am empowered to incorporate the message of salvation into everything I do. Some ways I have done this are teaching Bible studies and reaching out to people at my workplace, when walking in the grocery store, or even going to the doctors. My main reason for doing this is to nurture the growth of the church by expanding the body of Christ.

What about our families or those that we love the most? How do we follow this example of Jesus when we are around people who do not know Him or may even tell us outright that they don't want to know Jesus? I have been in this exact situation, and I looked to the Bible to help me in dealing with these tough questions. Paul explained it quite well in 1 Corinthians 2:4-5: "The message I preached and how I preached it was not an attempt to sway you with persuasive arguments but to prove to you the almighty power of God's Holy Spirit. For God intended that your faith not be established on man's wisdom but by

---

3. "Gregory the Illuminator," Wikipedia.com, https://en.wikipedia.org/wiki/Gregory_the_Illuminator, accessed June 4th, 2018..

trusting in his almighty power." I always keep it simple and bring my own personal relationship into the picture, telling what Jesus did for me.

My own family had several members who did not know Jesus in an intimate way. Because I daily pray for family members who are lost, the Lord always shows me ways to reach them. One day I was on the phone with my Armenian grandmother, who was eighty-eight years old and also a survivor of the Armenian genocide. I talk to her every week, but this day I felt a prompting from the Holy Spirit to share how much Jesus had changed my life after I asked Him into my heart. She started to ask me questions about my faith. My grandmother loved Jesus and she attended an Armenian Catholic church, but something in her heart yearned for the love I was speaking of when I talked about Jesus. Next thing I knew, she was expressing her desire to ask Jesus into her heart, and she wanted me to help her. Praise God, I led her in the prayer of salvation and she was saved. By the grace of God, we had four more years with her until she passed away and went home to be with the Lord. Being led by the Holy Spirit in every situation will take the pressure off of you and put the focus on Jesus. He will work through your heart and the hearts of others in order to reach the lost. Know that He has already equipped you to do this in your own family and beyond.

Chapter 5

Focus with Spiritual Eyes

Chapter 5

FOCUS WITH SPIRITUAL EYES

And you will open their eyes to their true condition, so that they may turn from darkness to the Light and from the power of Satan to the power of God. By placing their faith in me they will receive the total forgiveness of sins and be made holy, *taking hold of the inheritance that I give to my children*! (Acts 26:18)

Understanding Spiritual Vision

Spiritual vision occurs when God forms a picture in your mind of spiritual truths. If we think about physical vision, the stimulus for sight is light bouncing off physical objects. In spiritual vision, the stimulus for sight is light being reflected off spiritual realities. We need to understand that the light source for our spiritual vision is our Lord and Savior Jesus. What I want you to realize about spiritual vision is that those who have not asked Jesus to be their Savior are actually spiritually blind. This means the person has what I call "scales on their eyes" that prevent them from seeing the truth, because they have not asked Jesus into their heart. A great Bible verse that explains this is 2 Corinthians 4:3-4: "Even if our gospel message is veiled, it is only veiled to those who are perishing, for their minds have been blinded by the god of this age, leaving them in unbelief. Their blindness keeps them from seeing the dayspring light of the wonderful news of the glory of Jesus Christ, who is the divine image of God."

You see, the god of this age is Satan, who uses trickery, deceit, accusation, and slander to blind people's hearts. Therefore, when I witness to people I can tell right away who is blinded, and I never take offense to their negativity or animosity. Remember the verse in Ephesians 6:12 where it says, "Your hand-to-hand combat is not with human beings, but with the highest principalities and authorities operating in rebellion under the heavenly realms. For they are a powerful class of demon-gods and evil spirits that hold this dark world in bondage." Keep this verse in mind when you are speaking to people. It will help you recognize the truth in a situation as well as keep you focused on the Holy Spirit's direction for prayer.

Many times, we tend to look with our natural eyes to see what God is doing; however, the Lord wants you to look with your *new* spiritual vision once you have invited Jesus into your heart. In the natural, you may see your finances not accumulating, but as spiritual beings we are not to proclaim what we see in the natural but what we see with our supernatural eyes. This would mean for you to proclaim, decree, and declare that your barn is overflowing with blessings for you and your household. Jesus is the center of our focus and, therefore, if you are having problems seeing things with your spiritual eyes, you need to seek the source of all truth—Jesus. He is the one who can heal your heart and mend brokenness in your soul. If memories of your past want to stay present in your life, cry out to Jesus, who will come and bring you to the light. You will need to do something to be free to see with your spiritual eyes, and that is to ask the Lord to open your eyes to see Him and know His ways. I know this isn't always easy; but what is easier—to bring up a painful past memory so you can be healed and move forward, free from the chains that bind you, or to hide from your pain and never move forward, remaining bound to its effects?

Repentance becomes part of the picture in seeing more clearly with our heavenly eyesight. Repentance requires you to turn from your past sinful ways of living. I personally have had to repent for a lot of actions where I behaved sinfully, even as a born-again believer. There are many

Focus with Spiritual Eyes

actions that I have committed in which I operated out of my humanistic manners and not out of my spiritual being of truth. When God brings these things to your mind and you obediently come to Him asking for forgiveness, envision another scale being removed from your spiritual eyes that will never return, because now not only do you know the truth but you are inviting more of the light of heaven into your heart.

Keep Your Spiritual Eyes on God

Each day we have many distractions that solicit us to take our eyes off of what we need to accomplish for the kingdom. I am going to explain how our spiritual eyes are supposed to see, helping us know how to act. First, let me ask you a question. What kind of distractions are taking your spiritual eyes off of Jesus? Is it your work, family, or social activities? Personally, I have had all three of those try to distract me from walking with Jesus during my day. Therefore, I want to teach you what you can do to remove distractions in order to keep your spiritual eyes on the one who can clearly direct your steps.

The first thing you can do is get submerged into the Word of God. This will focus your spiritual eyes on His Word and His promises for your life. Would you believe without your vision being used every day, it can grow dark, or we can even become blind? In Revelation 3:17-19 we read that this is what happened to the church in Laodicea, which was the last of the seven churches Jesus addressed through John. The people actually thought one thing which was, in fact, very far from the truth. The passage reads, "For you claim, 'I'm rich and getting richer—I don't need a thing.' Yet you are clueless that you're miserable, poor, blind, barren, and naked! So, I counsel you to purchase gold perfected by fire, so that you can be truly rich. Purchase a white garment to cover and clothe your shameful Adam-nakedness. Purchase eye salve to be placed over your eyes so that you can truly see. All those I dearly love I unmask and train. So repent and be eager *to pursue what is right*."

We can understand from this verse how the church here did not see the truth of their circumstance. They really had no objective views of themselves or even of the true character of God. They also did not understand the way of salvation. I appreciate how in this verse they were told to buy eye salve so they could truly see and pursue what is right. There were many spiritual ailments this church was experiencing, but the first one mentioned is spiritual blindness. We are also not immune to this condition. In 2 Corinthians 4:4 we read, "For their minds have been blinded by the god of this age, leaving them in unbelief. Their blindness keeps them from seeing the dayspring light of the wonderful news of the glory of Jesus Christ, who is the divine image of God." In fact, every day we can read in the news what is happening around us that reveals the spiritual blindness the whole church is experiencing This verse explains how we can see desperation in the hearts of people in this world. As the "god of this age," or the enemy, can try to blind God's children and keep them in darkness, they will continue to see the world in a chaotic state. However, in verse 6 Paul states, "For God, who said, 'Let brilliant light shine out of darkness,' is the one who has cascaded his light into us—the brilliant dawning light of the glorious knowledge of God as we gaze into the face of Jesus Christ." What is most important here is how you and I can reverse this condition. As I mentioned earlier, you should be immersed in the Word of God. You can also stay free from blindness by spending time in worship and praise, as God is the One who will open your eyes and remove any blindness preventing you from seeing Him. Realize that Jesus is the only one who can supply you with an eternal inheritance, clothe you in righteousness, and heal you of spiritual blindness forever.

One can understand that without distractions, turmoil, or suffering it seems easy to keep your eyes on God. But what about those who have distractions that seem to never leave? Those who are victims of poverty and war, or who live in a country that does not allow them to read the Word of God or go to church. There are so many testimonies of people who have struggles but have kept their spiritual eyes on Jesus to bring kingdom expansion. One testimony that comes to mind is a woman who was a British missionary named Gladys Aylward. She traveled to China by train and boat across Europe and Asia. God protected her through many hardships and adventures during her worldwide trips. When she arrived in China, she helped an older missionary manage an inn where they would share Bible stories with visitors who just happened to pass through the area.

Focus with Spiritual Eyes

One of the local leaders decided to appoint Gladys as a foot inspector to help end the custom of foot-binding. The Chinese considered small feet to be beautiful, so preschool girls had their toes bent down under the soles of their feet and bandaged tightly to create smaller feet. The procedure was extremely painful and made it hard to walk normally. As a foot inspector, Gladys unbound the girls' feet and shared the story of Jesus with hundreds of Chinese people. Gladys also helped stop a prison riot, and through this taught the prisoners about Jesus, her first love. She was able to serve God in many other ways in China, because she was willing to be used by Him wherever He needed her. Gladys said, "I wasn't God's first choice for what I've done in China. I don't know who was. It must have been a man, a well-educated man. I don't know what happened. Perhaps he died. Perhaps he wasn't willing. And God looked down and saw Gladys Aylward. And God said, 'Well, she's willing.'" Because Gladys kept her spiritual eyes on Jesus, as a willing servant to the King, she was able to bring hundreds of people to Christ from the first day in 1932. Because of this, hundreds of thousands of Chinese people now know Jesus. As you keep your eyes on Jesus, believe that you can do this too!

Worldly Pull from Jesus

Have you ever heard of the devil being called Lucifer? He was an angel in the heavenly realm with God and other angels. The Bible tells us he decided he didn't want to serve God as the other angels did, but to have God serve him. Therefore, he was cast down to the earth, and the worldly system now displays that same kind of selfishness. If you read Ezekiel 28:11-19, it paints a picture of what happened to Lucifer. God loves all His creations and Lucifer was no exception. However, when he decided to turn from God, it clearly states what God decided to do: "Your rich commerce led you to violence, and you sinned. So I banished you in disgrace from the mountain of God. I expelled you, O mighty guardian, from your place among the stones of fire. Your heart was filled with pride because of all your beauty. Your wisdom was corrupted by your love of splendor. So I threw you to the ground and exposed you to the curious gaze of kings" (Ezekiel 28:16-17 NLT).

God on the Move

Because we have sin in this world, we are prone to follow it and its ways. However, that is not what the Lord has set up for His children. That's why we need a savior and why Jesus came down to save us from what sin has tried to do—separate us from God. The world always tries to entice people, telling them they need and want the latest and greatest "thing" to fill the emptiness in their soul. We see this in the news, through advertising, video games, the Internet and phone apps that lure children and adults, pulling at their heart's affections. At some point, a person will realize these things do nothing to fill them up and they will come seek out the light. For that reason, we as believers are commissioned to bring the light of Jesus to the world, knowing the only source who can fill them up is Jesus!

My own children didn't get cell phones until they were in high school, which caused them to be criticized and ridiculed. We live in an affluent region in Massachusetts, and most parents give their children cell phones in the fourth grade. I'm not talking flip phones either; these children have the latest and most expensive phones money can buy. Now, when you see or hear this, does it break your heart? It breaks mine, because the younger generation is getting more exposure to media through technology without the protection of their minds. As they see and hear things which are worldly, they start becoming followers of the world verses God's word which is truth. The saddest part is most of these parents themselves are embracing the ways of this world and are not teaching their children how to be equipped spiritually. In the book of Ephesians, Paul wrote a warning of how to be prepared for spiritual warfare in this world we live in.

Ephesians 6:11-13 tells us to, "Put on God's complete set of armor provided for us, so that you will be protected as you fight against the evil strategies of the accuser! Your hand-to-hand combat is not with human beings, but with the highest principalities and authorities operating in rebellion under the heavenly realms. For they are a powerful class of demon-gods and evil spirits that hold this dark world in bondage. Because of this, you must wear all the armor that God provides so you're protected as you confront the slanderer, for you are destined for all things and will rise victorious." I often say this verse over myself and

Focus with Spiritual Eyes

when I pray with my own children so they are also aware of what we as believers need to do to be equipped as we live in the world. I would encourage you also to continually put on the armor of God each and every day. As this verse states, we are not fighting with human beings or, as another version states, flesh and blood, but we battle powers that operate in rebellion to God. Know that the God of the universe wants you and your children to be fully armed, equipped, and ready.

While you live on this earth, God wants you to be a warrior for Christ. When you are at your workplace or in your neighborhood, you have choices that you can make that will allow others to want to embrace the love that you carry in your heart. It may not be easy at first, but remember that God is with you and you have the armor of God to protect you, so there is nothing to be afraid of.

To serve Christ fully we must overcome rejection in our own lives. Even Jesus Himself was rejected, as it says in Luke 4:16-27. Jesus came back to His hometown of Nazareth where He went to His synagogue. After He read from Isaiah and sat down everyone looked at Him. This is when He said, "These scriptures came true in front of you today." In verses 28-30, after hearing Jesus' first sermon, the people were very angry at Him. "When everyone present heard those words, they erupted with furious rage. They mobbed Jesus and threw him out of the city, dragging him to the edge of the cliff on the hill on which the city had been built, ready to hurl him off. But he walked right through the crowd, leaving them all stunned." If you personally have been rejected, I would urge you to sit with the Holy Spirit and find out where this spirit of rejection came from, as a spirit of rejection will make it difficult for you to move to the next level. If you feel you need deeper inner healing, there are many reputable, experienced ministers who can help walk you through the process of inner healing. What I want you to remember about any spirit not of God, is that He has given you all power and authority to trample over the enemy of this world. As His Word states, "Now you understand that I have imparted to you all my authority to trample over his kingdom. You will trample upon every demon before you and overcome every power Satan possesses. Absolutely nothing will be able to harm you as you walk in this authority" (Luke 10:9).

Jesus will always point you to the light while we live on this earth, and God has given us a choice of which way to follow. I personally tell my own children, "You can choose the ways of this world, which ultimately lead to darkness and sin, or you can choose the ways of heaven, which lead to peace and joy. The choice is yours." We all need the Lord in our lives and He will point us to the correct path. In Genesis 21:19, we read, "Then God opened Hagar's eyes, and she saw a well full of water. She quickly filled her water container and gave the boy a drink" (NLT). That's what we also need—for God to open our eyes so we can see the answer to our problems in His Word. This is what I ask of the Lord each day. I say, "Father, open my eyes so that I can receive sight from heaven and have your will be revealed on earth."

Petition or Supplication to the Lord

Don't you just love that we can go to God any time of day or night to seek Him and hear Him speak to us? It clearly states in Psalms 92:2, "At each and every sunrise we will be thanking you for your kindness and your love. As the sun sets and all through the night, we will keep proclaiming, 'You are so faithful!'" As we dive into why petitioning or supplication is so important to God, I want to help you understand more about what God's intentions were, as well as the prophets when they used this word in speaking with their heavenly Father. But first, I have a question for you. When I talk about petitioning the Lord, what comes to your mind? For me personally, I think about petitioning for a court to give custody over for a child or for some kind of judgment. Therefore, petitioning for something seems to be a word I would use when I need to go to someone and ask them something. Now, I want to flip this and have you think about heaven. Who in heaven can we petition for something? The simple answer is Jesus.

Merriam-Webster's dictionary states that a "petition" is a formal request. However, I want to switch gears and talk about the word that is used in conjunction with petition, and that word is *supplication*. In the English language we don't use this word very often. In fact, this word is from the fourteenth century in Middle English. The same dictionary defines

Focus with Spiritual Eyes

supplication as a humble request. When we think about petition and supplication, we can see what a difference there is in their meanings.

What is a prayer of supplication? "The Hebrew and Greek words most often translated 'supplication' in the Bible mean literally 'a request or petition,' so a prayer of supplication is asking God for something."[4] Supplication is one of several words in the Bible referring to prayer. The word is found sixty times in the Bible. It is a synonym of "prayer" and of the fifty-eight verses where supplication is used, thirty-one of these verses also have some form of the word *pray* or *prayer*. It also is meant to be used when describing kneeling or bowing down in submission, as Solomon did in 1 Kings 8.

Supplication seems to refer to the attitude or spirit of our prayer to God. Have you ever evaluated what your attitude is like when you are praying? I know for me as an entrepreneur, wife, and mother to three children, I find my supplications to the Lord occur when things seem to be falling apart in my family or work. However, there are also times in my day when I do feel I must go to the Lord requesting God to move in a situation. I can also petition Him to quickly move in a circumstance that is either affecting me or my family. Either way, it is a time I choose to seek the Lord. We know God examines our hearts when we go to Him in prayer. Many individuals in the Bible made supplication to the Lord. Let's discover who they were.

The first person I can think of is David. When he was writing to the Lord in the book of Psalms, you can feel how his words are filled with supplication for mercy. Later on, in the book of Daniel we learn how King Darius had issued an edict prohibiting prayer to any god but the king (see Daniel 6:9). Daniel continued to pray to God with prayers of thanksgiving as well as prayers of supplication for His help in this dire situation, which could have led to his death. Another example is when Jesus teaches us to ask for our daily bread in Matthew 6:11, which is a prayer of supplication.

---

4. "What Is a Prayer of Supplication?" Gotquestions.org, https://www.gotquestions.org/prayer-of-supplication.html.

God on the Move

As God moves, so must we come to Him through supplication, believing in Him and His promises as heaven collides with earth. What kind of requests are you making to God with supplication? Are you following along with the saints of the Bible and using Jesus' example? Clearly, prayers of supplication are part of the answer to our spiritual battles, which all Christians are engaged in. Paul further exhorts the Philippian church in Philippians 4:2-7, explaining to them how to relieve their anxieties by remaining faithful in prayer, especially prayers of thanksgiving and supplication. This, he concludes, is the formula for ensuring that "the peace of God, which transcends all understanding, will guard your hearts and your minds in Christ Jesus" (NIV).

Because we often don't know how to pray or what to pray for when we approach God, the Spirit of God intercedes and prays for us, interpreting our supplications. We read in Romans 8:26 how God makes this possible: "And in a similar way, the Holy Spirit takes hold of us in our human frailty to empower us in our weakness. For example, at times we don't even know how to pray, or know the best things to ask for. But the Holy Spirit rises up within us to super-intercede on our behalf, pleading to God with emotional sighs too deep for words." When we are overwhelmed by the trials and stresses of life, He comes alongside to lend assistance with our petitions and prayers of supplication as He sustains us before the throne of grace.

Chapter 6

Focus with Spiritual Ears

Chapter 6

FOCUS WITH SPIRITUAL EARS

My child, will you treasure my wisdom? Then, and only then, will you acquire it. And only if you accept my advice and hide it within will you succeed. So train your heart to listen when I speak and open your spirit wide to expand your discernment—then pass it on to your sons and daughters (Proverbs 2:1-2).

Train Your Heart to Listen

All my life, I have leaned into God to feel His heartbeat and hear His voice. This is His desire for His children: To continually have our ears attentive to His commands. Why do you think He designed us this way? My thought is that God designed us for His perfect will to be done on earth. Without spiritual ears you cannot hear His voice. Hearing is truly the understanding of something spoken and, in turn, being obedient to what you hear. As we listen to His voice as His sheep (see John 10:27) and not the voices of this world, we are moving more in line with His will and His ways instead of our own. I get lots of people asking me all the time, "Rhonda, how do you hear from God?" The first thing I ask them is, "Tell me how often you sit down to rest with the Lord."

In America, the word "rest" doesn't hold the same meaning as it does in other parts of the world. In fact, if you find yourself resting, you may hear someone ask you if you are lazy or just plain bored. We have been trained in this country not to rest or find time for ourselves. This is a lie from the enemy. Did you know on average, Americans take only one week vacation a year! In Europe, the majority of companies give their employees five weeks' vacation a year. Not only do they get this much time, but they also encourage time with family as a priority.

I started working when I was twelve years old. However, it wasn't until I met my husband, who is from Lebanon, that I learned the true meaning of the word *rest*. Work has been hard-wired into my brain from my upbringing and the world's perception of getting ahead. God, on the other hand, built in rest when He created us. He stated in the book of Genesis that on the seventh day, He rested. We read in Exodus 20:8-10, "Remember to observe the Sabbath day by keeping it holy. You have six days each week for your ordinary work, but the seventh day is a Sabbath day of rest dedicated to the Lord your God. On that day no one in your household may do any work. This includes you, your sons and daughters, your male and female servants, your livestock, and any foreigners living among you" (NLT).

Imagine, even the animals are commanded to rest on the Sabbath day. So where did we go wrong? When the enemy can get you to focus on something other than God, he will dangle it in front of you and try to convince you to keep your eyes on some false idol or prize. Mostly its money, pride, or jealousy. Money keeps you focused on wealth and what it can do. Pride helps you stay right where you are without moving forward, and you end up staying so consumed with yourself you end up taking God out of the picture. Jealousy is where you are constantly wanting what other people have. This demonstrates how we are not grateful for anything God has given to us. In all of these examples, you are tuning out your spiritual ears to God and tuning them in to the ways of this world. Therefore, I would highly encourage you to find rest in your day and be mindful of the ways the enemy would like to steal you away from your heavenly Father's presence. Resting and sitting at the feet of Jesus on a daily basis while reading His holy Word will train and prepare you to hear God's voice through your spiritual ears.

Focus with Spiritual Ears

Understanding Dreams

I have been a dreamer ever since I could remember. In the '70s and '80s, when I was growing up, there was a great movement of God, but there was also a great movement of new age and other false spiritual experiences, where people were guessing what was happening to you while you slept. Today, we have some very well-known and respected men and women of God we can watch through the Internet who can help us understand more about our dream meanings and how God wants to use our dreams for His purposes. We don't even need to leave the comfort of our homes. Through God's creativity, clarity will come to those who are searching for the truth, and I have discovered truth about the importance of dreams, which I am passing along to you.

We consider a dream to be a series of thoughts, images, or emotions occurring during the hours we sleep. A vision is something seen other than by your natural sight—it is seen by your prophetic sight. "Vision" also means the ability to see or plan something for the future. "Dream," on the other hand, is a state of being completely occupied by one's own thoughts. It is also the thoughts and pictures in the mind that come mostly during the hours of sleep. There are over 125 references to dreams in the Bible. This can be further broken down to twenty-one written dreams. Out of these, we find that six dreamers are kings, one is a woman (Pontius Pilate's wife, see Matt. 27:19), and two of the dreamers are named Joseph. With this kind of recurrence, we can sense God wanted us to recognize something significant related to the dreams we have today.

Therefore, how does God reveal Himself in our dreams? In my experience, I have found that when I am waking up from my dream, there are times when I remember exactly what the dream meant or who was in the dream. Nevertheless, sometimes I wake up and I can't remember anything other than that I had a dream. I have read from various teachings that the best kind of dream you can have is one you don't remember. This sounds counter-intuitive, but that is why God's Word is our source of truth. God says He will reveal what He has sealed away in your spirit according to His appointed time. We read this in Job 33.

God on the Move

> For God may speak in one way, or in another,
> *Yet man* does not perceive it.
> In a dream, in a vision of the night,
> When deep sleep falls upon men,
> While slumbering on their beds,
> Then He opens the ears of men,
> And seals their instruction (Job 33:14-16 NKJV).

Our dreams reveal God's directives and quite possibly the calling on our lives. Thankfully, the enemy of this world does not have access to our mind because we have been sealed by God (Ephesians 1:13-14) when we became born-again believers, and God is the only one who knows the future (Isaiah 46:9-10). Therefore, the only way your dream can be revealed to the enemy is when you open your mouth. As we read of Joseph in Genesis 37, we understand how his turn of events occurred once he shared the dream given to him by God. In Genesis 37:5-8 we read, "One night Joseph had a dream, and when he told his brothers about it, they hated him more than ever. 'Listen to this dream,' he said. 'We were out in the field, tying up bundles of grain. Suddenly my bundle stood up, and your bundles all gathered around and bowed low before mine!' His brothers responded, 'So you think you will be our king, do you? Do you actually think you will reign over us?' And they hated him all the more because of his dreams and the way he talked about them" (NLT).

If Joseph had simply waited to share his dream with his brothers and father, he may not have been sold as a slave and put into jail several times. Knowing the Lord entrusts to us certain messages doesn't mean we should be telling the world about them. In fact, the opposite is true. We need to ask God for permission before divulging any information to others. God often shares valuable information beforehand in order prepare us for whatever He has delivered to our spirits. Knowing the Lord is always preparing us for what is on the road ahead is important to keep at the forefront of our minds on a daily basis. God's eyes and ears are attentive to our prayers, so don't you believe He would want us to have the same attentiveness to His voice, as He's the one who created us? The answer is an astounding *yes!*

Focus with Spiritual Ears

Dreams are meant to be hidden in our hearts and pondered, for God will reveal the meaning at a later time. Therefore, we need to be in tune with God as He speaks to us to help us stay on the path that is part of our destiny. As we see in the story of Joseph, no one understood his dream, not even his father. Because of this misunderstanding, jealousy, rage, and unforgiveness began to penetrate the hearts of his brothers, which triggered a ploy to get rid of him and sell him off as a slave, then faking his death to their father.

We are to learn from this story and many others in the Bible. God will show us when to keep certain things hidden from the ears of man. Now, there are times we can sense there is a meaning or revelation in our dream that we do not understand yet, but a dream from God will always reveal something. Therefore, I want to encourage you to write down your dreams and visions. There are many times when the Lord will show you what your dream means to you. However, it may be months or even years from now. Just as the dream Joseph had did not come into fruition for many, many years, eventually it did come to pass, and so will yours.

If you're ever having dreams that are not encouraging, or maybe they are in black in white, realize that these dreams are not from God, but the enemy. The enemy of this world will try to produce fear in us, but God's perfect love will always cast out fear (1 John 4:18). Always remember your dreams must coincide with the Bible, as God's Word is the truth. You can also know whether a dream is from God based upon the results. Did this dream come to pass? Are there biblical symbols in your dream? Do you wake up with a sensation of the Holy Spirit being upon you? In any dream, one of the most important things you can do is to pray over your dream. When you do this, the Holy Spirit will begin to reveal more about your dream, often showing you where to look in the Word of God, bringing confirmation to your spirit and soul.

In Genesis 41:16, when Joseph was interpreting the dream for Pharaoh, we read, "'It is beyond my power to do this,' Joseph replied. 'But God can tell you what it means and set you at ease'" (NLT). Remember, it is God who interprets dreams. If God is using a dream to convey His message, then God should be our first source for interpretation. God does not keep secrets; however, you may have to search out the truths of what He is trying to convey. If He gave you the dream, He intends to also give you the full interpretation. The Holy Spirit is always looking for ears that will listen to what He is saying, eyes that will look at what He is showing, and hearts that will inquire after what He is thinking.

There are many ways God will speak to you during your lifetime. The most common ways He speaks are through dreams or visions. When you are dreaming, your mind goes into another world called the "dream state" or REM sleep. In Joel 2:28, God says, "I will pour out my Spirit upon all people. Your sons and daughters will prophesy. Your old men will dream dreams, and your young men will see visions" (NLT). I have been dreaming and remembering dreams my whole life. A few years ago, I started to write down all of my dreams and visions. It's amazing what God can reveal through dreams or visions. Surprisingly, we are more apt to listen to Him in a dream state or through a vision because His voice has such a profound effect on the mind. Whether it's through a dream or by way of a vision, God will get us to understand His message, which will undoubtedly shake our spirits to know it is Him. In doing so, we will embrace the message He is sending us in order to move closer to our destiny.

Hearing from God in a Vision

Let me help you understand how we perceive the Lord through vision. There are over one hundred references to the word *vision* in the Bible. The one verse that speaks to my heart is Numbers 12:6:

> And the Lord said to them, "Now listen to what I say: "If there were prophets among you, I, the Lord, would reveal myself in visions. I would speak to them in dreams.

If you receive a vision from God, it can come in the form of an audible voice, angelic encounter, heavenly encounter, or an actual open vision. I want you to know that nothing in your vision will contradict what the Bible has to say, and if it does, your vison is not from the Lord. I would like to share a testimony of how God has revealed dreams and

Focus with Spiritual Ears

visions to me. Several years ago, I was in a dream, and all of a sudden I heard the Lord's voice whisper to me. He said I would be writing a book. It was so early in the morning that I didn't know if I was actually dreaming or awake. When I finally opened my eyes, I knew I was now awake, but I could still feel the tangible presence of the Lord. In a gentle voice, I heard the Lord say again, "You will be writing a book and it will be called the Fifteen Steps to Evangelize." In this conversation with the Lord, I politely disagreed (not a good thing to do when the Lord is speaking to you) and I said, "How will I write a book when I am not an author?" to which the Lord replied, "I am the Author of your life." I quickly wrote this dream and vision down in my journal, which I still have today, and it is a reminder of the tangible presence of God in my life. Amazingly, the Lord gave me the download of all fifteen chapters in thirty minutes that very morning. The book was called *Jesus at Work: Simple Steps to Share Your Faith*. The Lord showed me this book will reach one million people during this great harvest, and all the glory goes to God for His dream planted within my heart!

While I was in worship at Patricia King's Women on the Frontlines World Convention, I had an amazing vision. A large part of having vision is sitting in worship with the Lord and having the Holy Spirit pour into you. In the stillness of those moments, you can have incredible visions from heaven. This is exactly what happened to me. As I was worshiping God, I was on my knees at the front of the stage bowing my head down in humility to the presence of Jesus. That's when a vision came to me. Jesus was coming down from heaven on a beautiful white horse, and an army of angels were around Him. I was so happy to be with Him. I hugged Him, embraced Him, and loved Him in that moment. He said, "Today I am going to crown you and your husband." Without delay, He put a royal crimson red velvet robe on both of us and then crowned us. He then brought us up a large staircase, and I asked Him about my children. Then, as I turned, I saw my oldest daughter Sophia dressed in a beautiful royal velvet sapphire dress, and on her head was a princess crown. My youngest daughter Ava had the same kind of dress and crown, but the dress was royal purple in color. My son Stefan was dressed in a prince's attire and he looked very regal. Jesus then said to Ara and me, "You two will now make *disciples of all nations*," and He waved His hand across the world where, when we looked down, we saw thousands of people. Wow, this vision rocked my world. I will never forget it, and it's not the only vision I've had where Jesus has crowned my husband and me. Remember, the Lord will confirm visions and dreams to you. This verse from James 1:12 really hit me after my vision of Jesus. "If your faith remains strong, even while surrounded by life's difficulties, you will continue to experience the untold blessings of God! True happiness comes as you pass the test with faith and receive the victorious crown of life promised to every lover of God!" Keep strong in your faith and be ready to receive the crown of life as you journey with Jesus, being alert with your spiritual ears to hear from God through the visions He sends to you.

Hearing from the Holy Spirit

Another way the Lord will speak to you is through the Holy Spirit. He is our counselor, comforter, and advocate. When Jesus was leaving His disciples, He wanted to encourage them and let them know they were not alone or without help in doing what they were called to do for the sake of Christ. In John 16:13-14, Jesus said, "But when the truth-giving Spirit comes, he will unveil the reality of every truth within you. He won't speak his own message, but only what he hears from the Father, and he will reveal prophetically to you what is to come. He will glorify me on the earth, for he will receive from me what is mine and reveal it to you."

This message is to encourage us as believers today as well. You and I are also disciples of Jesus, so God wants you to be encouraged by the Holy Spirit when you listen with the spiritual ears God gave you. Often, as I am praying with someone, I cry out, "Holy Spirit, come now and reveal the Father's plan to us as we seek His face to know His will in this situation." Many times, right after I pray, I get a vision of what our heavenly Father wants to reveal to this person. It usually ends in someone weeping, because when the Holy Spirit touches a person's heart it causes a person to have what some would call the "spiritual gift of tears."

Focus with Spiritual Ears

Tears or weeping is mentioned over 200 times in the Bible, and each time it is used powerfully by God. In Luke 7:38, we read about the prostitute who took her expensive alabaster jar filled with perfume and broke it to pour out onto Jesus's feet. "Broken and weeping, she covered his feet with the tears that fell from her face. She kept crying and drying his feet with her long hair. Over and over she kissed Jesus' feet. Then she opened her flask and anointed his feet with her costly perfume as an act of worship." Being in the presence of Jesus caused her to weep, and as she did her tears fell on His feet. This is how I feel when I get in the presence of the Almighty, as I am filled with the Holy Spirit. You become permeated with His love, and tears just flow so that you cannot contain them.

I have been to conferences where I am under the Holy Spirit's presence and something happens to me that I consider supernatural. At one conference, during the offering message, I heard the Lord speak to me to sow everything I had into this particular ministry. I had never done something like this before, nor had I ever heard the Lord speak to me in such a clear voice regarding doing this supernatural act of obedience. At first, I hesitated and even tried to deny that I heard the Lord speak to me about pouring out everything I had in my account to Him. Then, in my spirit, I knew I couldn't deny what I heard. I went up to the altar where the message was given, I held my arms up high, and said to the pastor (even though he wasn't looking at me), "I am giving this all to Jesus for my business, Royal Business Consulting!"

Two seconds later, I saw the pastor running down the altar to me, and next thing I knew I was on the floor shaking and crying. In this encounter, I fell under the presence of the Holy Spirit and the love of God poured into me to the point that I couldn't contain my emotions any longer. I think I must have stayed in this same emotional state for over thirty minutes. When the ushers picked me up and I went to my seat, I was still in the same condition, with love pouring over me—love so deep and so wide my tears wouldn't stop flowing. The amazing miracle wasn't just being under the presence of God, although this is a miracle in itself. The real miracle came when I finally stopped weeping and I noticed on the chair next to me an envelope, which was the same type as the one God had me use to put my money in at the altar. On the envelope was written "Royal Business Consulting." Inside the envelope was an amount of money I had never seen anyone "just give" to someone! The Lord spoke to my spirit immediately and said, "You cannot out-give me. Instantly, I can give you back what you sow into my kingdom for my sake."

This was one of the most amazing experiences I have ever had. I don't believe this would have happened if I had stayed in my seat and denied that the Holy Spirit was speaking to me. You too, can experience all that God has to offer when you obey His voice that comes through the ways He uses to get your attention—dreams, visions, angels, or the Holy Spirit, to name a few. It may be different for you, or it could even be a new way that I haven't mentioned here. However, if you obey His voice, keeping your spiritual ears attuned to Him, He will bless you and show you the way to walk on the path He has designed for you.

Chapter 7

WHEN GOD SPEAKS, DON'T KEEP SILENT

Chapter 7

WHEN GOD SPEAKS, DON'T KEEP SILENT

Every Scripture has been written by the Holy Spirit, the breath of God. It will empower you by its instruction and correction, giving you the strength to take the right direction and lead you deeper into the path of godliness (2 Timothy 3:16).

Don't Miss This Opportunity

When I was young, the most common story told in church was that of Moses on the mountain, where God reveals Himself to him for the first time with a burning bush. We read in Exodus 3:2, "There the angel of the Lord appeared to him in flames of fire from within a bush. Moses saw that though the bush was on fire it did not burn up" (NIV). Can you imagine having the Lord show up in a flaming bush and speaking to you from that bush? Never mind that you must remove your sandals in reverence for being in the Lord's presence. This same thing happened to Joshua where he needed to remove his sandals in the presence of the Lord out of respect for the King of kings (see Joshua 5:15).

How about you? Have you ever been in the presence of God and fallen prostrate to the ground out of reverence and respect for Jeshua? I have.

God on the Move

It was at another conference I was attending. We were worshiping the Lord and suddenly the Holy Spirit came down upon me and I felt so hot my face felt like it was literally burning. I started to cry, and the crying turned into hysterical crying until I could no longer sit, and I fell to the ground as my body started to shake uncontrollably. It was there that I saw Jesus looking into my eyes with the crown on His head, saying, "Do you love me, Rhonda?"

Yes, Lord.

"Do you love me, Rhonda?"

"Yes, Lord!" I said again with such passion. The questions reminded me of when Jesus asked Peter three times of his love for Him in John 21:15-17.

> After breakfast Jesus asked Simon Peter, 'Simon son of John, do you love me more than these?'
> "Yes, Lord," Peter replied, "you know I love you."
> "Then feed my lambs," Jesus told him.
> Jesus repeated the question: "Simon son of John, do you love me?"
> "Yes, Lord," Peter said, "you know I love you."
> "Then take care of my sheep," Jesus said.
> A third time he asked him, "Simon son of John, do you love me?"
> Peter was hurt that Jesus asked the question a third time. He said, "Lord, you know everything. You know that I love you."
> Jesus said, "Then feed my sheep" (NLT).

The love I felt in that moment with Jesus I will never forget.

What I experienced, and what Peter experienced, is how much the Lord loves us. God spoke to me and made my heart swell with love for Him. When God speaks to you it's important you respond to His request or you may miss an opportunity to encounter heaven on earth. Therefore, I feel this word is vitally important, because God never wants us to miss an encounter, which will happen if our heart is not acclimated to His.

Let's take a look at the life of Samuel and how he listened to the Lord's voice. During this time in history, the Lord rarely spoke to His people

When God Speaks, Don't Keep Silent

because their hearts were hardened to hearing His voice. When Samuel was just a small boy living with Eli and being taught by him, the Lord came in the night while he was sleeping (see 1 Samuel 3:2-4). At first, the boy did not recognize God's voice, so the Lord came back four times to receive the proper response from Samuel. God finally got the response He was looking for when Eli comprehended it was the Lord speaking. Eli told Samuel to respond by saying, "Speak, for your servant is listening." Isn't that the way we wish all conversations went? As I told you, I am a mother to three children, and often I have called to them for distinct reasons—dinner, bath time, taking the dog out for a walk, or just because I needed them. Do you think they respond in a way like Samuel? Nine times out of ten, I would say absolutely not. Now, think about how many times the Lord has tried to reach you like He did Samuel. How have you responded to His calling? It's not too late to say to the Lord, "Speak, your servant is listening."

There have been times in my life when the Lord has called me to do something extraordinary. His desire is for the kingdom to shine on earth; however, on many occasions I was too afraid to follow through or I would give the excuse to God that I didn't have the time and sometimes I missed the opportunity God had for me. One day I was dropping off a package to be mailed at the local shipping services store in my area. I know the owner of the store because I frequently use his services, and as always I like to say hello and ask him how he is doing. This day, however, I saw him walking from the back of the store to where I was standing, and clearly I heard the Lord say, "Pray for his knee." *Um, hello God, don't you know I am rushing around today and I only came in here quickly to drop this package off?* was my reply. I left and felt a sickness in my stomach for ignoring the Holy Spirit's prompting to pray for this man. Surprisingly, two days later my daughter had something for me to drop off again at the shipping store, which was highly unusual. I didn't even think about what God had said to me earlier until I walked into the store. Then it hit me, and the Holy Spirit again spoke to me, "Rhonda, pray for the healing of this man." Again, my stomach started to turn, and I made up excuse after excuse not to pray, saying things like, "There are people here, Lord, and he is so busy with all these boxes all around him he really doesn't have time for me to pray." After a few minutes, unfortunately, I left.

God on the Move

Three days later, someone else in my family had something for me to drop off at the same shipping store. Now this time, I remembered how I felt and what I missed by not obeying the voice of the Lord. I repented for my disobedience, and as I walked into the store, I knew I was to pray for the owner. As he took my package and said to me, "Anything else?" it was then that I had the boldness and confidence to say, "Yes, would you mind if I prayed for the healing of your knee?" Puzzled, he said, "Sure," and started to walk away. I chuckled at him and then said, "No, I would like to pray for the healing of your knee right now."

"Wow!" he said. "OK, sure." I prayed over him and specifically laid my hands on his knee (with permission, of course) and then I asked him to walk out what the Lord had wanted to give to him—freedom from pain. He seemed so joyful after that and thanked me for stopping in to pray for him.

How many times did the Lord speak to Samuel? He spoke three times till He came back for the fourth time and called his name again. How many times did the Lord speak to me? Three times till I finally said "yes." I love how the Lord is patient with His children as a father should be. A great verse that explains this so well is 2 Peter 3:15, "And keep in mind that our Lord's extraordinary patience simply means *more opportunity for* salvation, just as our dear brother Paul wrote to you with the wisdom that God gave him." Isn't this awesome, that our heavenly Father has so much patience and because of His loving patience there will be more salvations! We should really rejoice when we think of it this way. I am so thankful for a patient God who is willing to come back time and time again with the same question to prompt a reply. This obedient act of listening to God's voice continually brings glory to His kingdom in a greater way than we could ever imagine. Don't miss a heavenly opportunity if God speaks to you today. Press in, be brave, be courageous, and be bold for Jesus, watching miracles take place!

God's Instructions

The Lord also spoke directly to Saul of Tarsus on the Damascus Road. At that time, he was converted, and later came to be called the apostle Paul. We read in Acts 9:4-6:

When God Speaks, Don't Keep Silent

> Falling to the ground, he heard a booming voice say to him, "Saul, Saul, why are you persecuting me?" The men accompanying Saul were stunned and speechless, for they heard a heavenly voice but could see no one. Saul replied, "Who are you, Lord?" "I am Jesus, the Victorious, the one you are persecuting. Now, get up and go into the city, where you will be told what you are to do."

You can see through this verse how the Lord reaches those who are apart from Him. With love in His voice, He calls to them. In this verse we read that God wanted to know why Saul was causing such devastation in the church. However, He knew Saul's heart and reached out with love while he was on his journey of persecuting Christians and brought him back to the One he was running from. Saul was considered a "Hebrew of Hebrews." He also was a blasphemer of Christ and an oppressor of Christians. I think it's interesting how Saul, when spoken to by the Lord, says, "Who are you, Lord?" This shows us that he knew who was speaking to him, but I am sure that he had no idea the Lord God Almighty would call to him from the heavenly realms.

It is the same for us. Many of us are amazed to know the Lord would take interest in us and call us by name. This is what makes this verse so great for us as believers now. If you make a request to the Lord, we have confidence He hears our plea and will answer us. I love how God brings to the forefront the sin of Saul by revealing His knowledge of Saul persecuting Christians because they believed in Jesus. The same is true for us as believers. God will reveal the knowledge of our sin and gently tell us what to do next, just as He did for Saul. This is how much He loves us. He will highlight what we can do to change now.

God spoke to Saul, telling him to get up and go somewhere, where he would be given the next part of God's instructions. Have you heard from God in such a way that you only have part of the instructions, but if you don't follow in obedience you will not complete the full task that God has for you? I have! It happened to me when I was a professor at a college. I was teaching a science class. Before each class I would go to the copier room, where a man name José was always taking care of instructors' copying needs. This one particular day, I was even more excited about teaching and was always optimistic about what God would do when He showed up to my class. As I approached José this day, he seemed a little down. I asked him what was wrong, but he didn't want to share his worries with me. After I was done with my copying, I thanked him for his help and went on my way to class. As I was walking down the hallway to my classroom, in a clear and audible voice the Lord spoke to my spirit and said, "Go back there and ask him if you can pray for him." In my typical manner, I questioned and even argued with the Lord as I kept walking, because I was late for class. However, the Lord's gentle persistence won. As I approached the copier room again, José asked me why I had returned. I was quite nervous and not sure how I was going to approach him, but I said, "I know this sounds strange, but I have a great relationship with Jesus and He asked me to come back here and pray for you. Would you like me to do that?"

He looked at me with this angry and puzzled face, then said, "No, thank you." I couldn't believe it. I had purposefully stopped where I was going to obey God's instructions; why would this person say no! Now, imagine, I was late for my class and also utterly frustrated that God would ask me to pray for José when He knew his answer would be "No."

This is where some stories end, never knowing the reason why God instructed us to do something for His purpose. However, like Saul who only knew half of the instructions, I too only knew half of why I was called to do what I did for José. That is, until my class was over. One of my students approached me. She first started to talk about her trouble in learning biology, but then quickly changed the conversation to talk about her boyfriend who was abusing her and how her family didn't support anything that she did. I immediately went into prayer mode, asking the Holy Spirit for guidance on what to do for this daughter of the King. That's when I heard the Lord's voice again instructing me, "She is coming into my kingdom tonight. Share the good news." *Wow*, I thought to myself, *I barely know her, and I am just coming to know of this terrible situation she is in.* Again, with obedience to the Lord being the primary focus for everything I do, I let the Holy Spirit lead me to share the message of salvation with this young girl. After saying the prayer, she immediately started crying and hugged me, stating that she had not felt that kind of peace in her life, ever. From that prayer, I mentored her for a couple of months and not only did her whole family come to Christ, but she left her boyfriend, joined a church, and started a Bible study. Can you imagine what would have happened if I didn't obey the Lord and go back to pray with José? I believe God asking me to go pray for José was a test from the Lord. Would I obey His voice and stop what I was doing to do what He's calling me to? Personally, I think I would never have gotten an opportunity to witness to my young college student if I said no to Him. You see, God rewards our obedience and in turn this increases our faith to receive even greater revelation from the Lord.

Obedience to His Voice

I cannot emphasize enough the importance of being obedient when you hear the Lord speak to you. This is key to following His instructions. It is imperative for us to finish what God makes known to us, even though we may not know all the details or have the ending in sight. Knowing He speaks to you when He is ready for you to take action is significant in everything we do. That's why as soon as you hear Him speak, His only desire is for you to respond.

A verse that speaks to this way of communication is from Luke 11:27-28. Here, Jesus was speaking to a multitude of people and "a woman shouted from the crowd, 'God bless the one who gave you birth and nursed you as a child!' 'Yes,' said Jesus. 'But God will bless all who listen to the word of God and carefully obey everything they hear.'" Let's be the ones who are blessed by obeying this word from our sweet Lord and Savior, Jesus.

I am always accustomed to hearing from God, especially when I travel. This one morning, I stepped outside my hotel room and the woman who was cleaning our room was standing in front of the door. I said good morning to her and started to proceed down the hall to get breakfast. Just as I took about ten steps, I heard the Lord ask me to give her a prophetic word of encouragement. I took a few more steps and knew I shouldn't go any further, but instead turn around and go back to obey what God was calling me to do. I turned around and said to her, "I am a faithful servant of God and He asked me to pray for you today, would that be OK?"

"Oh, yes," she said, "that would be wonderful." I proceeded to pray for her and as I did, the Lord showed me things about her life where she needed encouragement. For instance, He told me she had a son and she was working that job specifically for him to have a better life. He told me that she had a Bible, but she hadn't read it in a while, and also that she used to go to church, but hadn't in a long while. Then, I told her that God loved her so much, He had sent me there that day to that specific room in order for her to know this. Tears were streaming down her face, and she looked at me and said, "How did you know these things?"

I said, "I have a great relationship with my heavenly Father and when He speaks to me, I obey His voice." We can see God on the move in this situation because I lived over 250 miles from this location and He put me there, in that hotel, to reach that one person because He loves her. I personally can't keep silent when God speaks, because I have witnessed many lives transformed by the power of God.

I have many testimonies like this one. However, there are also testimonies I personally have read that encouraged me early on in my walk with Christ. Have you ever heard of evangelist Reinhard Bonnke? He's an evangelist missionary to Africa. Early in his missionary walk, he was being supported financially by a well-known organization. One night he had a dream of a blood-washed Africa. He knew from this dream God was calling him to go and stay in Africa to see God's vision of salvations across Africa's continent come into fruition. However, when he approached the missionary support team about this idea, they flat out said no. He was in shock as he did not expect that answer. He was a young father with three small children and a wife to support. Clearly, God was calling him to Africa and the financial support for him and his family would not be available from his missionary support organization if he didn't follow their advice. As an obedient child to the King of kings, he decided to go into a quiet, remote hotel room and lock himself in there until he heard from God directly as to what direction to take. One decision would lead to financial stability, but in turn would make him a disobedient follower of Jesus. The other decision would make him an obedient follower, but would mean everything he earned would be from total dependence on God. As Reinhard pressed into the heart of God, he heard from Him after only a few hours of solitude. The Lord spoke to him, saying "Reinhard, if you don't go to Africa, I will choose someone else." The rest is history. Reinhard Bonnke is now seventy-seven years old as I write this book, and has advanced the kingdom of God by seeing over seventy-five million people make salvation decisions over the last three decades. In 2017, he returned to Nigeria to hold his Farewell Gospel Crusade, where he passed the torch to a younger generation of evangelists led by Bonnke's successor, Daniel Kolenda.

In these testimonies, God is revealing the importance of praying and seeking His confirmation in everything we do. His purpose will ultimately be revealed when we follow through in an act of obedience to His voice or word. Also, understanding that our ways are not God's ways is helpful when you are called to do something specific for His kingdom. Therefore, when the Lord speaks to you and tells you to do something, know that we may not have the full picture of His goals. Often it is difficult when God wants us to take action without fully understanding the "why," but the reality is that it's not important why, it's important to follow His instruction.

God shows us in His Word how we do not need to understand everything to follow the voice of the shepherd (see John 10:27). Knowing God will reveal, in His time, exactly what you need to know in order to operate from a position of faith and trust is the key point. Why do you think it's so critical in this season to hear God's voice? I believe it's because if we are willing servants to the Lord, then we need to know where our orders come from. His voice is what we should be listening to first in our day-to-day lives. You will have confidence when you learn how to distinguish God's voice from your own, and you will gain a clearer perspective on your calling and purpose. It is important to also recognize the ways the enemy desires to limit your hearing, even when God is shouting instructions to you, just as He did with Samuel and Saul. I pray you benefit from what you've learned, which will serve as your guide, recognizing the interferences trying to prevent you from hearing Jesus.

God on the Move

Then, you will do as all sheep that recognize their shepherd do—call to Him, follow His voice, and run into His loving arms.

Chapter 8

POSTED AT THE WATCHTOWER

Chapter 8

POSTED AT THE WATCHTOWER

> Then the watchman called out, "Day after day I have stood on the watchtower, my lord. Night after night I have remained at my post" (Isaiah 21:8 NLT).

Chosen to be a Watchman

When reading this verse in Isaiah, I had some questions to research for this book. Let's understand together what a watchman is and the role this person had during biblical times, as well as today. The Hebrew word for watchman is *tsaphah*[5] and it has the meaning "to lean forward, to peer into the distance; by implication means to observe, behold, spy out, wait for, keep the watch." The Oxford's dictionary states in the historical perspective a watchman is "a member of a body of people employed to keep watch in a town at night." Why would you need a watchman to stay day and night at a post? During biblical times these men were posted to keep danger, enemies, lions, or thieves from taking what was rightfully theirs. It was a very important role, and one that is not looked at very much today. Another word from Hebrew that is used is *shamar*,[6] which means "to guard, to keep, to be a watchman." What this word accentuates is the protective component of a prophet's mantle.

---

5. Strong's Concordance, H6822.
6. Strong's Concordance, H8104.

This role of preserving and guarding of the prophet's ministry is what every local church really needs. Pastors suffer unnecessarily because the office of a prophet has been misunderstood. The *shamar* characteristic of the prophet ministry is so crucial to the church today.

What's really intriguing to me is seeing how a watchman is highly desired by God. He uses the role of a watchman throughout the Bible, as we read in Ezekiel 3:17-19, where God gave a message through Ezekiel about his prophet's position and the importance of it in the eyes of God.

> Son of man, I have appointed you as a watchman for Israel. Whenever you receive a message from me, warn people immediately. If I warn the wicked, saying, 'You are under the penalty of death,' but you fail to deliver the warning, they will die in their sins. And I will hold you responsible for their deaths. If you warn them and they refuse to repent and keep on sinning, they will die in their sins. But you will have saved yourself because you obeyed me (NLT).

In this verse we begin to understand the watchman's role despite how people responded to the warning. If they heard the message, the prophet had done his job and was no longer responsible for the outcome. However, if the prophet did not deliver the warning, he also would be judged along with the wicked.

How about you? Could you stand day and night waiting for God's command? I know I have stood day and night waiting to hear from the Lord and His direction. Is it easy? No. Is the reward great? Yes. While I was employed at an educational institution, the Lord spoke to me telling me my time was ending as an employee there. When I heard from the Lord in this way, I got emotional and excited at the same time. I had been going through a lot of strife and hardship at this school. The leadership was unethical and dishonest, and the students were from impoverished areas, which meant they came to school with lots of burdens and strongholds. In other words, the battle there was excessive. One day, I was sitting in my office eating lunch and praying to the Lord when I felt this overwhelming love come over me. I remember physically holding up a tissue as a white

Posted at the Watchtower

flag and waving it above me to communicate to the Lord, "I surrender." What was I surrendering to? Well, when the Lord tells you that your time is up at a particular posting, the battles can become very intense. I wanted the Lord to know I desired to follow His will, and I was under His lordship and reign. After this act of surrendering to God, numerous students came to know Jesus, as well as educators. Then, in an instant, the Lord removed me from my watchtower. You see, the watchman's role is not only to keep watch or safeguard the area. Our role is bringing the message of salvation. It is also to bring the good news of Jesus to the world—or to the area in which God has commissioned us to be stationed. It is a privilege with great responsibility to be chosen as a watchman by God.

Waiting for the Lord to give you directions, or for Him to take you from your post, also requires great patience. Patience is something I'm always being tested with throughout my walk with Jesus, but God wants to encourage us from His Word regarding patience in 2 Thessalonians 1:4-5: *"We point to you as an example of unwavering faith for all the churches of God. We boast about how you continue to demonstrate unflinching endurance through all the persecutions and painful trials you are experiencing. All of this proves that God's judgment is always perfect and is intended to make you worthy of inheriting the kingdom of God, which is why you are going through these troubles."* This verse makes it evident how patience makes us worthy to inherit the kingdom of God. Does that mean it's simple or without difficulty? Certainly not. *The Passion Translation* footnotes for verse 4 explain, "No matter what difficulty we may pass through, a growing faith in Christ, an increasing love for others, and unwavering hope will be the keys to coming through it victoriously."[7]

Have you ever thought about the area you live in as a strategic place, planned by God for you and your family? God plans for you to intercede in your region because you are physically there and the light of Jesus lives within you. Maybe you're seeing sin run rampant in the local or national government. It may seem in the natural things are falling apart and there is no return from the path of destruction. However, this is the patience

---

7. *The Passion Translation®*, footnote for 2 Thessalonians 1:4. Copyright © 2017 by BroadStreet Publishing® Group, LLC. Used by permission. All rights reserved.

of a watchman—to intercede in prayer and in petitions and gather those around you to do the same. We are called to step in and move mountains by simply commanding them to do so. You may get frustrated at the speed you are seeing things move in the natural, but as spiritual beings we are not to look at the natural circumstances. We are called to behold supernatural acts of God's provision and intercession. You are chosen as a watchman!

Waiting as a Watchman

Why is it when our prayer isn't immediately answered we automatically think God doesn't hear us, or maybe that He doesn't even love us? I can't tell you how many people I have spoken to over the years who become weary in waiting for God's answer. Do you remember the historical ship that sank called the Titanic? The watchmen who stood waiting to warn the captain of any large glaciers took their eyes off the deep, dark ocean. Do you recall what happened to this monumental "unsinkable" ship? These watchmen were late in sending the warning message to the captain of the ship. Because of their lack of focus and other actions of people in charge, this sink-less ship sank to the bottom of the ocean.

Let's look back at our watchman in Isaiah 28. I'm sure this man had to have been chosen because of his personal record as well as how responsible he was in the region. However, while he was waiting in the watchtower, he also cried out for a response to his lord or employer who hired him to be there. Let me ask you a question. How long have you been waiting for an answer to come to you? Five years, ten years, or maybe twenty years? Let's be encouraged by what the Lord says in Acts 16:25-26 regarding our waiting, and see what praying and singing can do for our circumstance. "Around midnight Paul and Silas were praying and singing hymns to God, and the other prisoners were listening. Suddenly, there was a massive earthquake, and the prison was shaken to its foundations. All the doors immediately flew open, and the chains of every prisoner fell off!" (NLT). Sometimes, we continue to cry out to God for answers and feel they never come. Paul and Silas may have felt this way as well. But instead of wailing in their circumstance, they praised God and sang hymns in an act of worship. What a fitting example of what to do while we are waiting for God's answer.

Posted at the Watchtower

I know firsthand what it's like to wait on God and His answer. When I first started working in the biotechnology industry, there were a lot of things I needed to learn. For instance, I had to understand the role of my manager and how my work made her look good to her boss. What I didn't know was when things started to fall apart at this particular company, upper management was always quick to blame the lowest man on the totem pole—which was me. Upper management quickly tried to devise a plan to make me miserable in my position in order to make themselves look good. The work load they gave me was unrealistic and frankly quite wrong. As I cried out for a response from God, I wasn't hearing anything. I sought Him day and night to help me find a way to leave or find a new job to move to, but nothing came. As I endured this hardship, I learned a lot about myself and the people I worked with. This pain I was experiencing actually caused me to have empathy for those in leadership. Instead of being angry, I reached out in love to them and did exactly what they wanted me to do. When I started to wait as God wanted me to, all of a sudden a company I had interviewed with a few weeks earlier called me for a final interview. Within a week, they had hired me with more money and more flexibility. I was also given responsibility to not only conduct my own research, but I was put on all sorts of research papers where they honored the work I completed with some very well-known cardiologists in Boston. God knows how to move our hearts to be in line with His will. Don't look with weariness at your circumstance. On the contrary, look with your spiritual eyes and see the God of heaven and earth working behind the scenes to create the perfect path for you to walk in.

What do you think your reaction would be if God commissioned you to stand at your watchtower post day and night? If it's a new position, you could be fearful of missing what you were called to watch to begin with. You also could become weary in standing in this post daily with no signs of relief. What I want you to think about in regard to being a watchman is how this role is actually closely related to the role of a prophet. Let's see how these two roles intersect. First, a watchman is generally set high up in the region, or kingdom, in a tower. A prophet is also placed in an area where their calling is to bring warnings or news to the body of Christ. A watchman cannot be blind; they must have very good eyesight because they are posted to a position in which they need to see the danger coming and warn people. A prophet must also see clearly to discern what is happening in the world and in the church. They cannot be caught up in the developments of today's news, but they must persist to be clear and unyielding about the Word of God. In Proverbs 7:2 it tells us to guard the revelation-truth, which the Lord gives to us as believers: "If you do what I say you will live well. Guard your life with my revelation-truth, for my teaching is as precious as your eyesight." Revelation is seeing with your spiritual eyes and having visions from heaven that reveal insight into the future. This is why I said you cannot be blind as a watchman.

I understand the role of a watchman can be lonely because you may be in a place where you miss your friends and family or the ease of knowing how to do something. As we walk in this journey with the Lord, He is always raising us up to go to higher levels with Him in order to bring glory to His kingdom. Any new position I have taken has been lonely at first. I don't know people, or how the company works, and often I spend longer hours trying to learn how to work well in an unfamiliar environment. A prophet's life is also lonely. They not only have a high tower that separates them physically, but they are also separated spiritually by the elevated level of devotion to their calling. A prophet is often taken from the daily interactions of this world, which would distract them or cause their focus to be taken off of God and His voice. Maybe you too have been distracted by the ways of this world and are having trouble hearing the Lord's voice in the busyness of life. If so, I encourage you to look at the watchman's life and see how you can run to your watchtower in order to focus on God's voice and direction. Look at your current situation and believe in your heart that you are exactly where God wants you. You have a calling and purpose to be stationed in this location. Sit with Jesus to find out your orders while you are waiting and posted in this location. As you sit with Him, clarity will come to your heart and soul, aligning your personal destiny with heaven's scroll.

Chapter 9

No Shortage of Faith

Chapter 9

No Shortage of Faith

Every night and day we sincerely and fervently pray that we may see you face-to-face and furnish you with whatever may be lacking in your faith (1 Thessalonians 3:10).

Focused Faith

Faith seems to be one of the most talked-about gifts in the Bible. Abraham was one of the men in the Bible I think of so often when it comes to those who had astonishing faith in God. In Hebrews 11:17 we read, "Faith operated powerfully in Abraham for when he was put to the test he offered up Isaac. Even though he received God's promises of descendants, he was willing to offer up his only son!" This is a man who was totally focused on his faith in God. He did not waver in what God had called him to do, to the extent of actually being willing to sacrifice his own son. I'm not sure I would have this caliber of faith if I was tested in this way. Thank the Lord for His grace upon our lives, knowing if we are lacking anything, we can go to His Word, which provides the source of living water to refresh our lives.

When I worked in healthcare, there were things I did to step out in faith with Jesus every day. My office was a place where managers and employees liked to gather, so I prayed for everyone who entered to feel the tangible presence of the Holy Spirit. One day I was praying with a co-worker, and as we were praying I had a vision of us holding a night of worship with all of the Spanish-speaking employees at the company. Now, at this point, I thought there were only two people who spoke Spanish, because that's all I knew. However, when I asked him how many he knew, he said at least twenty. *Wow*, I thought, *this is amazing*. I prayed and asked God to give me courage to approach the people to invite them to what God showed me was to be called "A Night of Worship." A few weeks later, about twelve people came to the event (which was held in our conference room, with permission) and several people made professions of faith in Jesus. Holding this event took faith for me to step out and invite people to a Christian gathering. It took faith to believe God would bring them. After this event, people came to me for prayer, deliverance, and mentorship where they could develop a deeper relationship with Christ.

Webster defines faith as, "Firm belief, resting on probable evidence, in regard to important moral truth; That which is believed on any subject, as a system of religious belief; reliance on testimony."[8] However, the Bible defines faith in Hebrews 11:1, where it proclaims, "Now faith brings our hopes into reality and becomes the foundation needed to acquire the things we long for. It is all the evidence required to prove what is still unseen."

We may not see what God has in store for us, but as the Bible states, it is all the evidence we need to see God moving in our life. Throughout my own life, I have been tested in my faith walk with the Lord. There have been many times when I could easily fall prey to the devil's schemes. However, at each trial and temptation, the Lord has a promise for you and me if we keep strong in our faith. It says in James 1:3-4, "For you know that when your faith is tested it stirs up power within you to endure all things. And then as your endurance grows even stronger it will release perfection into every part of your being until there is nothing missing and nothing lacking."

So then, how does keeping our focus on faith increase the more we exercise it? Faith is the confidence in what we have hoped for; therefore,

---

8. Webster's Collegiate Dictionary, s.v., *faith*, (Springfield, MA: 1913, G & C. Merriam Co.).

No Shortage of Faith

when you do see your prayers get answered, your faith is increased for you to believe for bigger or greater things. Or as I like to say, my faith muscles get larger. My fitness recommendation for you is to start small in growing your faith. What this requires you to do is ask for something that seems trivial, but important to you personally; then watch and see God answer. Once your answer comes, then move on to a request that requires a larger amount of faith. Always remember, though, it is God's timing and not our own. Either way, you will start to see faith mount up inside of you to grow your faith muscles.

During my corporate career, I went through many job layoffs and trials over the years. However, there is one thing that stands out to me like a sore thumb. Each trial produced in me greater faith. I knew next time my faith muscles would be stronger to endure whatever came my way. Think of it like training to run a marathon. The person training doesn't just get up and run twenty-six miles one day. In reality, if they don't start training a year before their race, then they will most likely not succeed in completing what they set out to do, which is win! The same is true for you and me. We need to keep focused on our faith, running with Jesus each and every day.

Start using your faith muscles and build them up by believing in the vision or dream God gave to you. The most important advice I can give to anyone who is walking with the Lord is to not quit. Keep your eyes focused on the prize, which is Jesus, and your plans will always succeed. Seeing how God gives everyone the same measure of faith (see Romans 12:3), it is therefore up to you and me to grow it. If God gives it to you, then don't put it under dirt and bury it as the man did in the parable of Matthew 25:25. If you recall, the other men in the parable grew the money given to them because they had faith in what God was entrusting to their care. You can grow the gifts that God has placed within you simply by focusing on stepping out in faith.

Faith of the Disciples

When Jesus handpicked His disciples and started training them in exercising their faith, He taught them out of the Word of God. This is also how I operate in my training, and you should as well. Any teaching we do on a daily basis should come directly from the Word. We are so blessed to have the recordings of Jesus—the best teacher, mentor, friend, and leader who ever lived. He not only taught His disciples hundreds of lessons while He remained on earth, but He left us these lessons for us to learn from also. One that stands out to me as exercising the greatest measure of faith was when Peter stepped out of the boat during the storm.

In Matthew 14:25-31, we read the panic that set in for Peter and the disciples:

> At about four o'clock in the morning, Jesus came to them, walking on the waves! When the disciples saw him walking on top of the water, they were terrified and screamed, "A ghost!"
>
> Then Jesus said, "Be brave and don't be afraid. I am here!" Peter shouted out, "Lord, if it's really you, then have me join you on the water!"
>
> "Come and join me," Jesus replied. So, Peter stepped out onto the water and began to walk toward Jesus. But when he realized how high the waves were, he became frightened and started to sink.
>
> "Save me, Lord!" he cried out. Jesus immediately stretched out his hand and lifted him up and said, "What little faith you have! Why would you let doubt win?"

When Peter heard the voice of Jesus calling him to follow after Him in the water, his faith rose up so immensely it didn't matter how much rain, wind, or waves were around him, all he needed was Jesus. However, a few seconds later he started looking with his natural eyes at the same storm he had seen before he stepped out, and he started to sink. What was the lesson we learn from this example of Peter's faith? I feel it is to continue to listen for the Father's voice, even if everything around you looks like a storm. If you follow His voice to join Jesus, you won't sink. But, if you take your eyes off of Jesus and start to sink because of your

No Shortage of Faith

lack of faith, know that Jesus will stretch His hand out and lift you out of the storm to encourage you not to let doubt win.

Another example of the disciples stretching their faith was in John 6:5-6, where a crowd had followed after Jesus to hear Him speak. There were thousands of people wanting to hear the message. After sitting for such a long time, the people were hungry. Jesus Himself asked Philip a question to enlarge his faith, saying, "Where will we buy enough food to feed all these people?" You see, Jesus, who is the miracle worker and who already had done miracles before this event, was testing Philip's faith in order for him to be stretched. Did it work? I think it worked marvelously! Seeing two fish and five loaves of bread feed the multitudes carried the disciples a long way in their faith, I'm sure; I know this message has carried me.

The next morning after the disciples saw Jesus walking on water, they and the crowds went looking for Him. Even after He had performed many miracles, the crowds wanted more. Like most human beings, we are never fully satisfied unless we are full with the Love of Christ. We can assume this scenario was a great teaching moment for the disciples, as well as God's children. The question they asked Him in John 6:28 was, "So what should we do if we want to do God's work?" The response Jesus gave to the crowd as well as to His disciples actually offended them. In John 6:29, Jesus answered, "The work you can do for God starts with believing in the One he has sent." Because many people didn't like the answer Jesus was giving, and also because they lacked faith in Him, many of them left. However, it didn't matter how many left; what mattered was the message He gave to penetrate the hearts of those listening. All you need to do is *believe in Him*. Start with this and watch your faith increase beyond anything you can imagine.

Have you ever gotten offended because of the answer you received from God? Are you waiting for the effortless way in which God can fix your problem or situation? Let me assure you, God already knows this, and He is calling you to think in a new way and have faith in what He is doing in your life. Trust Him in the process of working out your problems and you will see a greater measure of faith rise up within you as it did for the disciples. All of this training was to prepare them for their destiny, and all of your training is to prepare you for your destiny, walking with Jesus every step of the way. We all should desire to be called faithful servants of God. As you step out of your boat—keeping your eyes on Jesus—you will see your faith rise up within you. In the end, my only desire is to get to the gates of heaven and have the Lord say to me, "Commending his servant, the master replied, 'You have done well, and proven yourself to be my loyal and trustworthy servant. Because you were faithful to manage a small sum, now I will put you in charge of much, much more.' You will experience the delight of your master, who will say to you, 'Come celebrate with me!'" (Matthew 25:21).

Standing on the Rock

Did you know a lot of Christians struggle with a lack of faith? The main reason for this is because we tend to follow our perceptions of what seems true rather than what we know to be true by faith. We follow what we see with our human eyes in the natural and tend to overlook the reality with our spiritual eyes. If there tends to be a lot of negativity around you, the atmosphere can absolutely alter the promise of God. I have walked into my workplace before with such amazing faith for the day and for what I was to accomplish for the kingdom. Then, I go into another room with people who don't have a relationship with Jesus and they put down every thought and idea I had. You can get very depleted if you are not standing on the rock, which is God's Word. When this starts to happen, I silently pray; and depending on how the Holy Spirit leads me, I may even offer suggestions that help these people to see with a new kingdom view. You may say to me, "Well, if they don't know Jesus, then how will they see with this viewpoint?"

Great question! God's word says in Romans 1:20 regarding everyone being without excuse, "*Opposition to truth cannot be excused on the basis of ignorance*, because from the creation of the world, the invisible qualities of God's nature have been made visible, such as his eternal power and transcendence. He has made his wonderful attributes easily perceived, for seeing the visible makes us understand the invisible. So then, this leaves everyone without excuse." When

No Shortage of Faith

you walk into a room, explain how to see the blessings all around them. Next time you or people you are around are tempted to fall prey to negativity because of the atmosphere around you, look up to the heavens and call upon your God to change the atmosphere you are in by His presence in you and watch what He does to increase your faith and joy.

If you want to know the greatest way to increase your faith, besides what I shared earlier, I would say it would be to spend more time with God, as it says in Matthew 14:23. If you continue to pray night and day, as Jesus did, you will start to see miracles manifest themselves right in front of you. Kathryn Kuhlman, a dedicated evangelist and revivalist, once said, "Faith is that quality or power by which the things desired become the things possessed." We can gain the things we desire because we are in line with what God wants us to possess.

I remember when I was new in this faith walk, my mentor and spiritual mother led me to test out my faith muscles by asking God for something and writing down what I was asking. I decided to create a dream or vision board because I am a visual learner. So I set out to pray about what I had dreamed about and to ask the Lord if it was in line with His will for my life at the time. I got out magazines and cut out pictures of everything I loved and desired with my heart.

Writing or cutting out photos and documenting your dreams or desires is a way of putting your faith in action. Through this, the Lord shows His children how much He loves them. I still have this dream board, and amazingly, everything I cut out as a dream or vision has come to pass. I remember I wanted so badly to have a Honda Odyssey minivan. I know what you're thinking, "Wow, that's how big your faith was?" The answer is yes. A Honda cost over forty-four thousand dollars, and at the time, with our income and raising three children under ten, it seemed completely impossible to buy. Would you believe in a few months, a close relative of ours sold some property and gave us money that allowed us to buy the car I had faith to own? There were more amazing things that came to pass in this vision board, but the point is I had it written down and now I am telling you in order for you to be encouraged and not lacking in your faith.

In Habakkuk 2:2-3 NLT it says:

> Then the Lord said to me,
> "Write my answer plainly on tablets,
> so that a runner can carry the correct message to others.
> This vision is for a future time.
> It describes the end, and it will be fulfilled.
> If it seems slow in coming, wait patiently,
> for it will surely take place.
> It will not be delayed."

I recommend you do an experiment to test your own faith and try this out for yourself. I guarantee your faith will no longer be lacking, but instead it will be rising! Knowing God wants us to remember what He has done for us, we need to therefore keep a record of what we have seen Him accomplish. Write in a journal, keep a word document in your computer, or share your testimony with a friend. All of this builds up not only your faith, but the faith of those around you. Let's look together at the life of the disciples to learn how Jesus helped them grow in faith. Then we can truly understand by following the greatest teacher who ever lived and we will never have a shortage of faith while we live on this earth.

Chapter 10

SERVING THE BODY OF CHRIST

Chapter 10

SERVING THE BODY OF CHRIST

For this reason, they are before the throne of God, ministering to him as priests day and night, within his cloud-filled sanctuary. And the enthroned One spreads over them his tabernacle-shelter (Revelation 7:15).

Does God Need Us to Serve?

When Paul was speaking to the leaders in Athens regarding their worship of idols he made it very clear to them there is only one true God. "The true God is the Creator of all things. He is the owner and Lord of the heavenly realm and the earthly realm, and he doesn't live in man-made temples. He supplies life and breath and all things to every living being. He doesn't lack a thing that we mortals could supply for him, for he has all things and everything he needs" (Acts 17:24-25). God doesn't need us, but He created us for His pleasure. What this means is, whatever we do, we are ultimately doing it to share His glory with those around us.

Because God created us for His pleasure and we know He is love, then serving Him is an act of love. Let's look at the people of Athens to whom Paul was speaking. These were intellectuals who had built their history around idols and gods. Did it do them any good to worship idols when the time came for their death? This is one of the reasons Paul was to go to Athens—to share the good news of Jesus with these intellectuals in hopes they would drop their religious views and gain a relationship with Christ. Because I currently live in the state of Massachusetts, I feel there is a great comparison with the people here to the region of Athens during Paul's time. Currently, Massachusetts ranks as the number one most intelligent state in the union and is considered the most intellectual out of all fifty states. Pew research conducted a study to find out the religious profile of the fifty states. Their study found Southern states to be the most highly religious states in the nation, while New Englanders are the least devout. In my opinion, this study shows the more educated your state is, the less likely you are to rely on the God who gave you your intelligence.

One of the reasons I believe God has placed me here in this region is not only to share the gospel with these incredible intellects, but also because I speak their language. My personal salvation testimony has changed more lives than I can count. You see, intellectuals cannot debate your own encounter with God, because it's your encounter. I serve the Lord daily by showing my neighbors, my co-workers, and the people in my community His love. By doing this they are gaining a personal interaction with their heavenly Father. It's undeniable when you encounter the love of God. This is what changes nations. This is what transforms lives. Love.

However, before you can serve God, He needs to be able to pour into you as an empty vessel. The emptier your vessel is, the more the Holy Spirit can fill you up to overflowing. How can God fill something that is already filled? He can't. Therefore, as your empty vessel receives from Him, you will be filled to pour out in the areas He is calling you to without possible recognition or acknowledgment from anyone you are ministering to. I have always said to my Father, "Lord, let them see Jesus in me and not Rhonda, so that they know it is you who brought these things into fruition." God doesn't need us to serve; He wants us to serve. To do this, we must be emptied in order pour into the location He has strategically placed us in. By doing so, you will be changing not only the atmosphere around you, but a whole region or nation!

Serving the Body of Christ

Jesus Trains Us to Serve

In reading the New Testament, I learned the simplicity of sharing the gospel message. How I did this was by simply studying how Jesus trained His disciples and taught them what they were to do when He was called to leave this earth. As I explained previously, Jesus taught His disciples through spending quality time with them on a daily basis. Throughout the New Testament, Jesus had the disciples watch Him as He was teaching a crowd in a message, healing the sick, or raising the dead. After only a few years of training, it was time for Jesus to leave them on their own to lead their own people in the same way they were taught. Some would call this an impartation. An impartation gives us the ability to do in the natural realm what would ordinarily not be possible. This can only come through faith as a result of Jesus' work on the cross, which not only gives us salvation and everlasting life, but the power to miracles, signs, and wonders. It's a supernatural manifestation of the power of God.

Through this impartation, we have what some call the "The Great Commission." At one point, I thought this term was what Jesus expressed as His command to the disciples. However, this is not true. This term was coined from a Dutch missionary, named Justinian von Welz (1621-1688); however, it was Hudson Taylor who actually made this term popular among Christians over 200 years later. In the book of Matthew, Jesus is speaking to His leaders on what to do next, as they had completed their training. When the disciples met Jesus at the mountain, we read in Matthew 28:18-20, "Then Jesus came close to them and said, 'All the authority of the universe has been given to me. Now go *in my authority* **and make disciples of all nations, baptizing them in the name of the Father, the Son, and the Holy Spirit.** And teach them to faithfully follow all that I have commanded you. And never forget that I am with you every day, even to the completion of this age.'" In essence, Jesus is handing over His power and authority, leaving them the Holy Spirit to guide them. He commissioned them to do what He Himself was called to do by the Father, and now, as believers and followers of Christ, we are also commissioned to do the same.

God on the Move

We can serve the Lord daily and learn from Jesus' teaching, which shows us exactly how to do this in our own lives. I personally serve God all the time by seeking His will, reading His Word, and executing my orders for the day. All the while, I am giving Him the glory. You may be able to relate to my next real-life testimony of serving God with my family.

As I have shared, I have three children. A few years ago, my oldest daughter was getting ready to choose a college to attend for four years. If any of you have ever experienced the ebbs and flows of preparing your child to leave for college you will empathize with me. As I continually searched the Lord's heart on where exactly God wanted my daughter to be, it seemed clear. We had already visited four colleges. Two were in Massachusetts, one in Canada, and one in California. My husband was adamant on her staying close to home because of the difficulties children face when they first leave home. I agreed with this; however, I also believed wherever the Lord wanted Sophia He would be the one to show her and would give her father and me peace about this decision. As Sophia got closer to her decision, the enemy would creep in and begin to set fears in my heart about her being far from home and the things that could happen. When this occurred, I had to run to my prayer closet and search God's Word for the truth, just as the disciples had to do when they went to the ends of the earth proclaiming the gospel message.

The night Sophia made her decision, she was fighting with me because she wanted me to make the decision for her. Don't we all want God to make decisions for us at some point in time? It would be easier for us not to have free will, but God did not design us this way. I knew in my heart God was going to gain her trust in the calling on her life, if He was the one who spoke to her. I said to her, "You need to make this decision with God. He will direct your path and show you which way to go. He will give you the peace you seek in this choice." A couple of hours later, she came downstairs in tears, holding the sticker of Azusa Pacific University in her hand. She said the Lord told her this was where she was to go, and He would be with her every step of the way! We all cried together, praising God for His answer to prayer with our daughter.

As husband and wife, it is important for us to serve the Lord in everything we do. How we accomplish this in our marriage is by letting Him lead

Serving the Body of Christ

our children on the path they are destined to take. Sometimes, it just isn't that easy. Knowing that our children are a gift from God essentially means they are on loan to us. I can testify, three years later, how amazing my daughter's walk has been. God took her to school 6,000 miles away in California—a school whose mission has been "God First" since 1899. The university's values are grounded in "Christ, Scholarship, Community, and Service." Praise the Lord for His answer to prayer, all because we put Him first. Not only has she has been on mission trips to Mexico and served in China, but as I write this she is now headed on another mission trip to Greece, where she and her team will bring the gospel message, just like Paul did in the book of Acts. Always remember, when you put God first He makes a way in the wasteland and streams in the desert for His loving children (see Isaiah 43:19). Peter explains, in 1 Peter 4:11, how serving God is our ministry while we are on this earth. He states, *"For example*, if you have a speaking *gift*, speak as though God were speaking his words through you. If you have *the gift of* serving, do it *passionately* with the strength God gives you, so that in everything God *alone* will be glorified through Jesus Christ. For to him belong the power and the glory forever throughout all ages! Amen." As you journey with Jesus, may you seek to serve Him with all your heart, soul, and mind (see Matthew 22:37). Jesus said this is the greatest law, and we know by obeying this law blessings will certainly follow you all the days of your life.

Trusting God While Serving

Christ has come to show us how to serve the body of Christ. The word *serve* as defined by Webster is, "to work for; to labor in behalf of; to benefit."[9] Therefore, if I am a servant, then I am carrying out an act of kindness to someone. God designed it this way because serving is a moment-by-moment receiving from God's abundant supply of love. We receive this supply of love *by faith*. Meaning we trust God moment by moment and, by serving Him, we know He will supply everything we need.

---

9. Webster's Collegiate Dictionary, s.v., *serve*, (Springfield, MA: 1913, G & C. Merriam Co.).

God on the Move

If you are a wife and mother, then you are serving your husband and family. If you have a job outside the home, you serve your manager by completing the tasks given to you in order for the company to succeed. I remember when I was a young mom, I went to a mom-to-mom support group where I learned about who God wanted us to serve first. The leader taught us that we are first to serve the Lord and His kingdom. We do this by honoring Him and obeying His Word. Second, we are to serve our family. When I learned of this teaching in my late twenties, I was new to the idea of not serving myself first. I mean, let's be honest—in America, selfishness is promoted every day in advertising and the media, as well as in our school systems. I thought, *How can I serve God before serving myself? Who's going to take care of ME!* This began a process of deep introspection in my soul, contemplating God's way versus "my way" (as Frank Sinatra used to sing).

Years later, I was invited by my own church to be the women's ministry leader. At this point, I had grasped the idea of serving God and family, so I leaped at the opportunity. I had always prayed about serving God in the church, and I also felt it was one of the highest honors. Before I asked anyone or even prayed about it, I said yes! I couldn't wait to serve my church and the women of my church. During this period, I used to meet monthly with my spiritual mentor. After I got offered this position, I went to her office and we were praying about everything God was opening up for me in the church. As we prayed and invited the Holy Spirit into our conversation, she asked me one simple question. As I pondered this question, my whole life seemed to flash in front of me.

She asked me what my husband felt about this offer to become the women's ministry leader. I laughed and said, "My husband? I never asked him because I know God is calling me to this position." She gently and quietly explained to me that if I planned on leading other women in how to put God first, then family, I would need to show other women how to put their family first before ministry. I said I would pray about this and ask the Lord to show me when to open the topic to my husband. Three days later, the Holy Spirit led me to ask my husband about whether he felt this was what I should be doing. To my surprise he said he was so happy I decided to ask him this question. Then, he went

Serving the Body of Christ

on to explain how we had three children under the age of seven, and I was working almost thirty hours a week. How would I have time to give 100 percent to my family and have leftover time for the demands needed to build up this ministry? I cried for over a week about my decision to say no to the church's offer. However, this decision was probably one of the best decisions I have ever made, because I listened to God, and my husband, putting my family first. Blessings started to happen all around me. My marriage began to flourish even greater than before, and my children were so happy to have me available to spend time pouring into them during their adolescence. I trusted God while I was serving my family, and so should you.

When Joshua summoned all the tribes of Israel and explained the blessings God had given to them over the years, he explicitly stated they must choose whom they will serve:

> So fear the Lord and serve him wholeheartedly. Put away forever the idols your ancestors worshiped when they lived beyond the Euphrates River and in Egypt. Serve the Lord alone. But if you refuse to serve the Lord, then choose today whom you will serve. Would you prefer the gods your ancestors served beyond the Euphrates? Or will it be the gods of the Amorites in whose land you now live? But as for me and my family, we will serve the Lord (Joshua 24:14-15 NLT).

As God's children, we need to choose whether we will serve the Lord or the world. It's quite simple—we will serve one or the other. Joshua explains that no matter what, he will not follow or be influenced by other people and the way they do things. We too need to remember whom we are serving. Know that your choice may not be a popular one, or even one that is accepted by society. But let's thank God we are not looking to impress men or the world we live in. The only way blessings will come to you and your household will be from trusting, honoring, and serving the one true God.

Chapter 11

EMPLOYED BY GOD

Chapter 11

EMPLOYED BY GOD

Beloved brothers and sisters, surely you remember how hard we labored among you. We worked night and day so that we would not become a burden to you while we preached the wonderful gospel of God (1 Thessalonians 2:9).

Equipped to Go!

When we are in tune with God's plan, He will equip us to go forth with energy and enthusiasm. We have so many amazing examples of how to live our lives as ministers of God's Word. I think Paul said it best in 1 Corinthians 9:16-18:

> For you see, even though I proclaim the good news, I can't take the credit for my labors, for I am compelled to fulfill my duty by completing this work. It would be agony to me if I did not constantly preach the gospel! If it were my own idea to preach as a way to make a living, I would expect to be paid. Since it's not my idea but God's, who commissioned me, I am entrusted with the stewardship of the gospel *whether or not I'm paid.* So then, where is my reward? It is found in continually depositing the good news *into people's hearts*, without obligation, free of charge, and not insisting on my rights to be financially supported.

God on the Move

When the Lord called me to go into full-time ministry several years ago, I had no idea what this meant. Mind you, I was already doing ministry work at my corporate job, sharing Jesus and holding Bible studies for more people to come to know Him. But when we read this verse, we understand a little bit deeper about God commissioning you out of your job and taking you to a brand new mission field. I could not boast about the labor of my work to anyone because each day that I woke up, it was just me and God. As I have stated earlier, He is my CEO and most trusted confidant. I have learned a lot about being employed by God over these last few years. As Paul so eloquently stated, "I am entrusted with the stewardship of the gospel whether or not I'm paid." My payment comes from hearing the multitude of testimonies from the people God (my VP of Marketing) puts me in contact with for His glory. For this, I am extremely joyful to have leader like Jesus who gives me creative ideas as well as the gospel to feed upon daily. I would like to reiterate Paul's words, "It would be agony to me if I did not constantly preach the gospel!" Glory to God, I am in a country where I am free to do this.

Unfortunately, we live in a world where a lot of people are looking to be rewarded for their virtuous deeds in sharing the good news. I have been made aware of new ministries launching, but in observation with the years that pass, see there is no fruit being revealed. Now, I'm not implying their ministries are not meant to spring forth; I'm simply seeing some ministries with improper foundations. Many believe that money should be constantly poured into their ministry from donors, even though their mission or vision is totally unclear. Or some feel that individuals should be serving full-time in their ministry, even though the ministry is not clear on its focus. Either way, when there is no fruit being produced, we should always look to see if we forced the seed through the soil ourselves. We can push the seeds we have through the fertile soil, but eventually without water the seed will die.

Many times, as humans, we tend to get carried away when a prophetic word is spoken over us, telling us to "go and preach to the nations"; we can get excited about the word without listening to God's directive. The reality is, no one can commission you but God. As Paul says in this verse above, "where is my reward?" The reward is not in financial gain, titles, power, or status. The reward is found in sharing the good news of Jesus with the world while we are here. This is a privilege and blessing.

As you are being equipped to go where the Lord leads, remember this verse in Galatians 1:10 as an encouragement to you in following God versus man: "I'm obviously not trying to flatter you or water down my message to be popular with men, but my supreme passion is to please God. For if all I attempt to do is please people, I would not be the true servant of the Messiah."

Continue to trust God to provide for your ministry calling and have faith in His plan for your life, knowing faith is one of the greatest currencies we have on earth. God will always equip you before He sends you. As CEO of your life, remember that He will never leave you or forsake you.

Planted to Prosper

Working for the Lord means whatever we do, we do it for the Lord and His kingdom. Any place of employment He places you in is an opportunity for ministry growth and kingdom expansion. There are many people who are just waiting for God to take them to their ministry or final destination where they can be happy in what they are doing. As I have stated before, God has placed you where you are today and that is exactly where He wants you! I had this same feeling of wanting to be at my final ministry destination a few years ago. During that time no one ever said to me, "Rhonda, have you ever thought this is where God wants you to be?" On the contrary, most people said they would pray for me and the desires of my heart. That was until I cried out to the Lord and asked Him about the ministry I had desired all my life. Then I heard His voice loud and clear in my spirit and His direction became clear. He said, "Where I have called you to be today, Rhonda, is exactly where you are stay until I call you elsewhere." This word excited my spirit, as I felt I was finally converging with my destiny. What was so amazing to me was that my ministry was right in front of me all the time. My spiritual eyes had finally been opened to what God was doing in me every day of my life. I was serving Him in my place of employment, and this was my ministry.

God on the Move

I believe God doesn't want us to separate our ministry from our jobs. In fact, I feel He wants us to always be serving Him by showing others, no matter where they are, God loves them and wants a relationship with them. God is on the move each day in our lives, we just need to open our spiritual senses to His presence.

So where does God have you right now? Has someone prophesied over you, saying you were called to the nations, but instead you're cleaning houses? Or has the Lord given you the desire to start a non-profit to help women, but instead you're an accountant in a lawyer's office? These are all good and valid thoughts which should keep you focused on the Lord while encouraging you to press forward. I would like you to start looking at your current circumstances as your ministry and calling. Whether you see it or not, your "nation" is right in front of you, and there are so many people who need your help today. God surrounds you with people who need the light of Jesus. You are the light of the world because you carry Jesus within you, so you are more than qualified to spread this light. Start to flip the way you think about your current situation and see the positive in where you are. Begin to thank God for placing you in this place you occupy. You will kindle the spirit within you to share love with the world when you give Him praise and glory in your circumstance. Remember, any job you ever possess, the Lord is with you. His plan is always to prosper you when you are in line with His will (see Jeremiah 29:11). Serving others in the capacity which God places you is, in fact, serving God. The fruit of the spirit begins to bloom when you demonstrate the love of the Father.

Before I had children, I obtained my BS degree in pre-veterinarian science and worked at several pharmaceutical companies. Thankfully, God doesn't look at what my resume looks like. He also doesn't look at our resumes to qualify us for His work. We can see this by looking at all the people He chose in the Bible. Abraham, Moses, and David were all shepherds before God called them to lead His chosen people. Deborah was a woman who had never led an army before, and Mary was very young when she conceived Jesus. My point is, God doesn't look at whether you're qualified; He calls you because He has a kingdom plan. In Exodus 4:11-12 it says, "Then the Lord asked Moses, 'Who makes a person's mouth? Who decides whether people speak or do not speak, hear or do not hear, see or do not see? Is it not I, the Lord? Now go! I will be with you as you speak, and I will instruct you in what to say'" (NLT). As we look at His plan it will usually require supernatural faith to step out and do what God is calling you to.

Several years after receiving my degree and working in my field, I had two small children at home. I decided to take a job at a Christian school as a kindergarten aide. At this time my daughter and son were attending the school and it made the most sense for us as a family. I considered this job easy and non-challenging work compared to my previous years in research, but nonetheless I knew God wanted me planted here. Each day, I would always finish my job early. Instead of sitting and twiddling my thumbs, I went to the principal's office and asked her if she needed help. She gave me lots of busy-work at first. Then, when I finished, I asked again what else I could do to help her. When she finally realized my qualifications, she asked me to help her create a website for the school. In my time there, I went from being a kindergarten aide to becoming the principal's assistant (unofficially). God isn't looking for whether you are qualified or not. He is looking for people who will bear great fruit by obeying His voice, being humble, and serving Him, as Paul mentions in Colossians 3:23. You see, God's call on your life is not about you; it always has been and always will be about Jesus.

Tentmakers Like Paul

Would you believe there are tentmakers roaming the earth today just as in the days when Paul worked in this profession? There are organizations whose main goal is to help Christians become tentmakers. You might ask, what is a tentmaker? They are Christians who are missions-motivated, who support their families by secular work while doing cross-cultural evangelism while they are on the job, as well as in their free time. You could be a tentmaker right now. As I explained earlier, serving God where you are planted is exactly what He wants us to do. You could be working at a store today and show someone kindness by smiling at them, asking them how they are doing, or even asking if you can pray for them. Evangelism is done while we are working a full-time job, part-time job, or if we are at home. I don't believe God ever said sharing the gospel was to be a separate task from our day-to-day life; however, somehow this is the way it has evolved over the years. In Paul's life, for example, we can see how he took his skills and used them to advance the kingdom.

Just how effective was Paul's strategy in all of this? Let's take a look at all that he and those he trained accomplished. To give a picture of what Paul was working with, he had trained laymen who were from unpleasant, uneducated, and even pagan backgrounds. Most of these people were actually slaves. Yet they had received the gospel at great personal risk, and they risked their lives without pay to take it to others. In ten years (the three journeys took a decade) Paul and his friends—without financial support—evangelized six Roman provinces! How did they do this? By winning the hearts of largely uninformed converts, most of whom were slaves in their region. Paul's tent-making business was created to support his missionary work, but he didn't need to separate the two in order for him to succeed, because God blesses those who share the love of Jesus with those around them.

The key point to remember is to make sure your current work lines up with your calling, gifts, and passions. As God wants the desires of your heart to be fulfilled, He never said in His Word to do something you hate because you need to make money to support your ministry. In fact, there should be no separation between your work and your ministry. As we are united under God, so should be the work we complete while we are living and breathing on earth. It is also important to remember the scripture tied to everything we do: "Let every activity of your lives and every word that comes from your lips be drenched with the beauty of our Lord Jesus, the Anointed One. And bring your constant praise to God the Father because of what Christ has done for you!" (Colossians 3:17).

We know from reading about Paul's life as a tentmaker evangelist that he never wanted to be a burden to the church or to those he came to serve. What this means is he never wanted to become dependent on anyone but God to provide for him. Did you know Paul never allowed the churches he helped launch to become dependent on foreign funds or even on foreign leadership? Paul's business strategy was not accidental.

Employed by God

He knew if he didn't show in his own ministry an example to others of what it was like for a person to support himself, he would not be able to launch self-supporting evangelists or even independent churches. What intelligent thinking from a remarkable leader!

Do you think we personally burden the church when we are working in full-time ministry? The answer is no. Paul's example shows us this, as well as the example we have of Peter, who relied on the gifts of the church to support what God was calling him to do. When you are called, God has already set the stage for you and has already equipped you with the tools needed to accomplish His goal. All you need is faith to accompany the calling.

Working in the Corporate World

The marketplace is an incredible avenue for Christians to serve because the majority of unbelievers never even enter a church. If you think about the effect you have on people every day in your place of work, it's not surprising how important it is for your light to shine and for people to know of your faith in Jesus. The majority of your time is spent at your place of employment; therefore, don't you think—as you speak to others—that the importance of your words to a hurting world can mean the difference between life and death?

When I was working at a healthcare company, I would be praying for my manager and all of the people on my team. One day, my boss looked so stressed and overworked. I prayed at my desk, asking the Lord to give me a word for him. The word God gave me was Philippians 4:6-7: "Don't be pulled in different directions or worried about a thing. Be saturated in prayer throughout each day, offering your faith-filled requests before God with overflowing gratitude. Tell him every detail of your life, then God's wonderful peace that transcends human understanding, *will make the answers known to you* through Jesus Christ." I left this verse on his desk, and when he came back from lunch, he picked it up, read it, and then immediately came over to me. I didn't know what he would say, and quite honestly I was a little nervous. However, when God gives you directions or directives and you follow them, He will bless whatever the outcome may be. My boss said that no one had ever given him a

Bible verse before, and even though he was Catholic, he didn't know any Bible verses himself. To this day, when we meet for lunch, he talks about how much this verse meant to him and the relationship he has with God for the direction of his life.

Christians in the marketplace played a vital role in the emergence, establishment, and expansion of the early Church—in fact, most of Jesus' followers remained in full-time business while simultaneously conducting full-time ministry. This was possible because they saw the marketplace as their parish and their business as a pulpit. To them, witnessing was not an occasional activity but a lifestyle. What a fantastic way to approach our work and ministry. Not as two separate establishments or jobs, but one work under one amazing God. If you think about it, work is a part of God's original design for the human race. Just by looking at the life of Jesus' ministry, we can see how He focused on the marketplace, where people spent most of their time. He roamed the streets and went to establishments where business people were. He didn't wait for people to come to Him, but instead He sought out those people in order to give them a touch from heaven. I truly believe God has clearly given us a directive to expand the gospel message in our daily lives. As you watch God on the move in your own life, don't wait for people to come to you, but seek them out as the Holy Spirit directs you and watch God do the rest. A great verse that will help you is from Colossians 3:23: "Put your heart and soul into every activity you do, as though you are doing it for the Lord himself and not merely for others." This year, I would like to challenge you to look at your work as one ministry for God and under God. Let's witness together revival happen in all seven mountains across the earth.

The Union of Day and Night

Do you find your home to be quiet in the morning? When my children were young, morning was the only time there was no quietness. I remember them waking me up in the middle of the night or early hours of the morning to climb into bed with my husband and me. It seemed the night hours were the only time we had peace, because they went to sleep in their beds. If you have young children, you understand the moment they go to sleep, you feel this strong pull to also climb into bed and slip into your own deep slumber of exhaustion.

I love the Psalms, because they tell us how Jesus is there for us every morning and every night. We read in chapter five, verse three: "At each and every sunrise you will hear my voice as I prepare my *sacrifice of* prayer to you. Every morning I lay out the pieces of my life on the altar and wait *for your fire to fall upon my heart.*"

As my children grew older, I savored the early morning hours as a chance to wake up and spend time in silence with my heavenly Father, because my night time was spent with teenagers till the wee hours of the morning. Don't get me wrong; I loved each of these phases with my children. At each phase I knew it was precious time to be savored. Currently, as I write this book, my oldest daughter is still in college in California, my middle son is graduating high school and preparing himself to leave home for his new adventure with God, and my youngest daughter is getting ready to enter high school. I am so thankful God gave me three children, because each child has their own giftings and uniqueness about them. How quickly you can go from it never being quiet in your house to a home with no children and complete silence. Whether you have a home with or without children, God is with you in your silence or your chaos. Whether night or day, all you need to do is take time to sit with Jesus. In either atmosphere you will see what He wants you to do as He moves through your life.

When thinking about the union of day and night, there are over thirty-six verses in the Bible for us to read about the morning hours. Why do you think the Lord would want to reiterate this point so many times? If we look at what happens in the morning on a typical day, we can start to understand the importance of the morning hours. First of all, after a good night's rest, where your body has had time to rejuvenate new cells and clear the mind of the previous day's thoughts, we are able to receive additional information into our minds. In essence, your mind is fresh and free of stress. The quietness of the day brings newness to our thoughts for wherever God is taking us.

God on the Move

> But whenever you pray, go into your innermost chamber and be alone with Father God, praying to him in secret. And your Father, who sees all you do, will reward you openly (Matthew 6:6).

When you are employed by God, it is important to wake early in the morning, as you can withdraw from the noise that will quickly try to steal your dreams and plans. As I wake up early in the morning, I look to God for directions throughout the day. Asking Him what He wants me to do becomes a dialogue with Him. I feel in our conversation we always come to a happy compromise. There are many people in the Bible who also "arose early in the morning" in order to accomplish a plan. For instance, Moses climbed Mt. Sinai early in the morning with the tablets in his hands as the Lord commanded (see Exodus 34:4); Joshua led the Israelites across the Jordan River as he rose early in the morning to direct them (see Joshua 3:1); David rose early in the morning and slayed the giant Goliath (see 1 Samuel 17:20); and very early on Sunday morning the women followers of Jesus arose to anoint His body with spices (see Luke 24:1).

Seeing God move is easy when you start your day focusing on Him and His plans. The things you talk about or the requests you have for His help become obvious. You can celebrate God's goodness when you know He is for you and with you throughout the day. Romans 8:28 explains this. "So we are convinced that every detail of our lives is continually woven together to fit into God's perfect plan of bringing good into our lives, for we are His lovers who have been called to fulfill His designed purpose." We can pray, *Lord, increase my resolve to pursue only what you call me to do, and deliver me from the fragmenting effect of fruitless distraction.*

As well, we can look at how God spoke many times during the night, understanding the equal importance of this time of day. In Acts 18:9, God visits Paul to encourage him. "One night, the Lord spoke to Paul in a supernatural vision and said, 'Don't ever be afraid. Speak the words that I give you and don't be intimidated." Bear in mind, most of our dreams occur during the night, and visions can come at the end of day when our minds are in a resting state. We realize when we are employed by God, how He uses time for His divine purpose of joining together what He created at the beginning of creation—night and day. Throughout this book, I pray the Lord revealed to you how a pillar of cloud by day and a pillar of fire by night was a gift from God to the Israelites and to us. The purpose was to guide, protect, and increase our faith to trust in Jesus more each day. Be assured that the angel of God goes before you and will move you out of the wilderness. Through this movement, you will see Jesus manifest Himself to you through this cloud and fire. Let me close with this verse from Galatians 6:22:

> "But now, as God's loving servants, you live in joyous freedom from the power of sin. So consider the benefits you now enjoy—you are brought deeper into the experience of true holiness that ends with eternal life!"

Believe with your eyes of faith that you were created to do what Jesus did while on this earth. You are meant to move with God and you are empowered to do what Jesus did, night and day, day and night.

About the Author

RHONDA KITABJIAN is an entrepreneur, educator, author, and speaker. She has a master's degree in education focused on organizational management and is the founder and president of Royal Business Consulting (RBC). She imparts wisdom, simple strategies and laser focus for leaders to change the world for Christ through their business or ministry.

Through RBC, Rhonda provides godly counsel to entrepreneurs, discerning each strategy tailor-made by God to transform an organization. Therefore, if you are ready to build a successful business or ministry, Royal Business Consulting will uncover your true potential, execute in your vision, and assist you in fulfilling God's plans for your business.

Rhonda has more than twenty-five years of corporate experience as director of products, manager of scientific research and as a sales executive. She has been responsible for directing and managing the business and product strategy at several large profile corporations.

Rhonda is known for her positive and uplifting demeanor, which encourages leaders to become more focused and effective in their roles. No matter where she has been employed, her main focus has been and always will be Jesus. This is the main reason for her continued entrepreneurial success.

To book Rhonda to speak at your next business or faith-based conference or to find out more about her products or services, you contact her at www.royalbc.co or by emailing info@royalbc.co.

You can also visit her YouTube channel for encouraging business insights: Rhonda Kitabjian or visit her Facebook page: www.facebook.com/royalbusinessconsulting.

CPSIA information can be obtained
at www.ICGtesting.com
Printed in the USA
LVHW08s0131051018
592385LV00021B/720/P